The Game Changer

Lane Walker

LOCAL LEGENDS
www.bakkenbooks.com

The Game Changer by Lane Walker
Copyright © 2023 Lane Walker

Cover Design: Roger Betka

All rights reserved. This book is protected under the copyright laws of the United States of America. This book may not be copied or reprinted for commercial gain or profit.

ISBN 978-1-955657-88-4
For Worldwide Distribution
Printed in the U.S.A.

Published by Bakken Books
2022
www.bakkenbooks.com

*This book is dedicated to all the kids
who have ever felt alone…
You are not alone; you are somebody,
and you are loved!*

Local Legends
The Buzzer Beater
The High Cheese
The Storm Blitz
The Last Green
The Game Changer

Hometown Hunters Collection
Legend of the Ghost Buck
The Hunt for Scarface
Terror on Deadwood Lake
The Boss on Redemption Road
The Day It Rained Ducks
The Lost Deer Camp

The Fishing Chronicles
Monster of Farallon Islands
The River King
The Ice Queen
The Bass Factory
The Search for Big Lou

For more books, visit: www.bakkenbooks.com

- 1 -

Prologue

The soccer game was tied 3-3, and the two teams were engaged in a shoot-out to determine the winner.

"Tank!" Coach Newton yelled, turning toward the bench.

"I think Coach is calling your name," said a teammate sitting next to me on the bench.

"Oh, no. Are you sure?" *Coach had said this couldn't happen.*

A sudden silence went over the crowd as I glanced back toward the soccer field. My mind was racing, trying to figure out exactly what I was going to do.

Not now—not in a game like this.

I hadn't played a single second in a soccer game—ever! The magnitude of the game caused me to scrutinize the field and my opponent ever so carefully.

Our goalie, Chris Smith, was doubled up in pain, holding his ankle. In the intensity of the game, I hadn't stopped to think of the ramifications when Chris went down. Obviously, he had severely injured his ankle on the last play.

"Tank! You're up!" Coach yelled again.

I stood up. I knew I had to go in, but I had never expected to play in the championship game.

I didn't want to play, which might sound odd to those champing at the bit to play.

I was only on the team because I had made a promise, and Tank Armstrong always kept his promise…*but now?*

Now I was expected to go into the game and help my home team, the Golden Tornadoes, win their first regional soccer championship. The hopes of our entire town rested solely on my shoulders.

The Game Changer

My attempt to jog onto the field felt more like I was staggering. I was trying my best to hide my anxiety and lack of confidence. My whole life had been spent making sure other people saw me as a good athlete. After all, I was large and slightly overweight for my age.

My size was what had originally drawn me to the football field. Coaches loved my size, and my teammates loved running the football behind me. Being big and quick were two great characteristics to have on the football field.

At only thirteen years old, I had already played four years of organized football. I was a captain and one of the best players in the area. Only now I wasn't on the football field…at least, not my definition of a football field.

None of that mattered now; the only matter of importance was doing my best to help my teammates win.

My knees started to shake, and my hands were getting wet with sweat as I took my place in front of the large net.

Lane Walker

Why couldn't I have been a forward or a fullback? Why did I have to be a goalie? I thought to myself.

Goalie is the one position on the field where a person couldn't possibly hide. The goalie could make a game-saving play or be the reason why his team lost a match.

I could feel the weight of everyone staring at me. I glanced back over my shoulder and saw all my football buddies with their mouths hanging wide open. Not one single person had expected me to play today.

"Tank, you got this!" I recognized a familiar voice with a distinctive Spanish accent. I looked back at the field, surprised to see Marco smiling at me. "I believe in you," he encouraged.

I smiled at him, trying to reflect his confidence.

In truth, I had only been on the team for a week. In spite of an occasional gym class, soccer remained a weird, new sport to me.

The only thing on my mind at that moment was that the eight by twenty-four-foot soccer net no

The Game Changer

longer looked big. In fact, it felt like it was closing in around me.

I looked around one more time at the large crowd and my teammates.

Instead of being outside standing in a huge soccer goal, I felt like I was trapped—caught in a small room with the walls slowly closing in around me.

-2-

Growing up in Union City, Tennessee, has been a great experience. The population of 11,000 people or so has always seemed like just enough and not too many. Another element I love about Union City is its diversity. My city is home to many different ethnic groups, and everyone seems to get along and treat each other with respect.

Even though I had never lived anywhere else, I am still certain Union City is an awesome place to call home. The town received its name in 1852 from General George Biggs because of the two railroads that connected in the settlement. The Northwestern Railroad out of Kentucky and the Alabama/Ohio Railroad shared a "union" or in railroad terms, a *junction* at that very spot. The union of these two important tracks made Union City a fitting name for the growing settlement.

Someone outside of Tennessee would probably have never even heard of my town if not for a couple of tourist attractions. The first is a world-renowned museum called Discovery Park of America, located on Reelfoot Lake, offering 100,000 square feet of historical artifacts and over fifty acres of park and adventure.

The second thing Union City is known for is football. Though my first love was baseball, I soon changed my focus to football. As soon as I started playing pee wee football in the third grade, I wanted to play for the Union City Golden Tornadoes. The only colors that mattered from that moment on were the purple and gold of our high school uniform. I will never forget the first time I pulled on a football helmet.

My grandpa would often tell my dad, "Tommy is a born football player; he is built like a tank." My body has always been thick and solid, and I was very strong for a thirteen-year-old boy. I also had big hands and feet, so my dad thought I would do well as a basketball player. I liked to hoop, but my true passion was on the gridiron.

From a young age, I knew I was different. I was always the biggest kid in my class. In fact, I remember one time in second grade we had a substitute teacher, who took one look at me and then sent me to the office. She was convinced I was a fifth grader playing a joke, trying to take advantage of her. Our principal, Mr. Aarons, politely invited the sub to step into the hallway with him, while he sent me back to class.

Not long afterward, the red-faced substitute teacher returned to the classroom. I could tell she was embarrassed. She came to where I was sitting and apologized, but I wasn't upset; I was used to people thinking I was older than my classmates.

The first time I stepped onto the field, I knew I was made to play football. On the football field, everything felt natural to me.

By the time I was in fifth grade, I was nearly six

The Game Changer

feet tall—five foot ten inches to be exact. Weighing around 180 pounds, I dominated on the football field and quickly found success. Due to my unusually large size, I was used to people looking at me quizzically. However, my size wasn't the only aspect that made me stand out.

My dad is African American, and my mom is from Brazil. My skin color is light-brown due to my unique parentage, and this often makes me stand out.

All too soon, I was entering eighth grade ready for my final year of middle school football. After this year was over, I would finally get my chance to suit up for the Golden Tornadoes high school team. I was blessed to have some other really good football players in my class. Many of the local folks, who had been around Union City football for a long time, felt like our team had all the makings of future state champions.

Union City has won three state championships in the school's history, but our last victory was over twenty years ago. Our first middle school game was two weeks away. We knew a ton of fans would come out to support our team. As a matter of fact, the fans in Union City pack the stadium for every football game, not just high school.

After an undefeated seventh-grade season, our whole team felt like another perfect season was just beginning.

In Union City, we didn't hope to win. We expected it.

-3-

During the second week of school, something happened that would change my life forever. The question is whether the change would be the good kind or the bad kind.

I remember sitting in math class when I saw Mr. Hawkins, our school counselor, and Mr. Aarons, our principal, look through the small window in the door. They appeared to be talking to someone and motioning toward our classroom. I watched as the door slowly opened.

Mr. Simpson, our math teacher, immediately stopped talking and looked in their direction. I was surprised to see only our principal enter the classroom.

"Excuse me, class," Mr. Aarons announced loudly. "I would like to introduce you all to a new student who will be starting at Union City Middle School today."

We looked around, but nobody was there. Mr. Aarons could tell something was wrong and also turned. He walked back out into the hall, where we could hear him talking to someone.

Then a small, skinny kid with long legs stepped into our classroom. He was below average in size—much smaller than I was. And his skin was a lighter shade of brown than mine.

"Class, this is Marco Santiago. His family moved from Barcelona, Spain, to Union City this week," introduced Mr. Aarons.

The new kid stood there with his head lowered, looking utterly embarrassed. Mr. Aarons had no idea that he was actually making things worse for the new kid. I could tell Mr. Aarons thought his introduction was helping, but he was unintentionally making an awkward moment even more uncomfortable for an eighth grader.

The Game Changer

"Go ahead and sit right here, Marco," said Mr. Aarons as he motioned for Marco to take the only open seat—the one directly behind me.

Clearly, Mr. Aarons didn't realize that the seat behind me was always open because no one liked sitting there. My size made it hard for the person sitting there to see anything.

Marco quickly sat down, trying to escape the unwanted attention.

Mr. Simpson went right back to teaching his math lesson as 30 eighth graders stared at the new kid.

After a couple of minutes, I could hear some whispers to my left. I turned to see Bobby "Biff" Taylor mouthing something toward Marco. Biff was a running back and linebacker on the football team. A fairly good player, he was strong for a thirteen-year-old.

Two details stood out about Biff. First, he loved to eat. He ate everything in sight and was even known to walk up and grab food off other kids' plates in the lunchroom.

Biff was also known for picking on and teasing everyone around him, especially the smaller or quieter kids. He bullied everyone, using his overbearing size and weight to do what he wanted around school. My larger stature seemed to make it easier for him to be nice to me.

Biff and I had become reasonably good friends over the past four years—mostly because we shared a love for football. On the football field, Biff was a great teammate and worked hard to win. However, when he was around the other kids during school hours, he acted like a completely different person.

I began watching the encounter and saw a confused look on Marco's face as Biff kept whispering in his ear. I finally had enough and made eye contact with Biff. Once our eyes locked, he quickly got the hint and stopped talking.

After that, we had about ten minutes of peaceful study time before the bell rang. As soon as the students heard the bell, they knew it was time to eat lunch. Half of the kids in class ran out Mr. Simpson's door toward the lunchroom. Some of

The Game Changer

the other eighth graders played a game to see who could get in line the fastest. I was fast, but not nearly fast enough to compete with them. Plus, today was meatloaf day so I knew plenty would be left by the time I made it to the lunchroom.

The other half of the kids made a beeline toward Marco. Whenever a new kid moves into our school, a wave of excitement floods the building.

I chuckled to myself as I watched. The sight reminded me of bees flocking toward their beehive. I wondered if Marco wished he could swat and shoo them away.

I gathered my books, but Biff's voice caught my attention as I walked by the mob in the hallway.

"Good news, we got ourselves a football star!" Biff exclaimed in his deepest voice.

Marco grinned as he exclaimed, "Yes, yes, football! I like football." I knew he was in big trouble as soon as I heard him talk. He couldn't speak English very well, and his strong accent revealed he was used to speaking Spanish.

Biff put his arm around his shoulders and

grinned. "We are always looking for a football star around this school," he said in a scoffing voice.

I shook my head and walked out. Clearly, Marco had no idea with whom he was talking, and Biff was up to no good.

I walked down the hallway toward the lunchroom, wondering if Marco really was good at football. *Another great player would only make our team better.*

He did seem to get really excited when Biff said "football." Maybe Marco could be good for Union City.

-4-

The initial buzz around the new kid was starting to wear off as I entered my sixth hour physical education class. I hadn't seen Marco in any of my other classes the rest of the day and had pretty much forgotten about the new kid from Spain.

That scenario all changed when I walked out of the locker room and jogged toward the football field. The first thing I noticed was a small group of students near the south end zone. I looked around for Mr. Gomez, our P.E. teacher, but he wasn't outside yet.

As I jogged toward the group, I could hear laughter. I recognized most of those involved; they were on my football team. I could hear Biff's deep, booming voice before I saw what was going on. *Whatever is happening can't be good.*

I pushed my way through the crowd of onlookers and saw Marco standing in the middle.

"Let's try this again, Marco," Biff yelled as he hurled a football at Marco's head. Marco ducked and tried to get out of the way, but the ball hit him directly in the back of the head, knocking him over.

The boys laughed.

Marco tried to shake off the jolt and hop up quickly, but clearly he was a little unsteady as he almost fell over again.

I stood there staring, not sure what to do. This wasn't an easy position for me. Most of these guys were my friends and teammates. I had known them for years and wanted them to like me. I loved being part of a team—being one of the guys working together on the football field.

"Football, but not this kind of football," Marco managed to sputter as he got back on his feet.

I looked to my right and noticed Eddie Robinson was recording the encounter with his cell

The Game Changer

phone. Eddie was our quarterback and one of the most popular kids in the entire school. Eddie is a good guy for the most part, but at times he drove me nuts. He was best buddies with Biff, and when those two were together, they acted differently. They always wanted to show off and act cool.

When I first met Eddie and Biff in fifth grade at football practice, I didn't like them. In fact, I still remember their making fun of me for being so big, but that was four years ago. Since then, we had become friends, and they had stopped teasing me. They respected me and my ability on the football field.

It seemed like Marco couldn't catch a break. *What a terrible first day for him!*

First, he had been embarrassed by Mr. Aarons in front of our whole math class, and now he was on the wrong side of half of the football team. The only thing that shut Biff up was when Marco mentioned football.

Biff walked over and picked up the ball, handing it to Marco.

The way Marco held the ball sideways made it obvious that he had never carried a football in his life.

"So, you are a football star, huh?" Biff sneered.

Biff was feeding off the other boys' jeering and laughing.

"No, no, no star," answered Marco in broken English.

That Marco wasn't a football player was now apparent to all.

"Run past me and try to cross this line," Biff said as he pointed to a large white line a couple feet behind him.

Marco looked at Biff then at the ball with no idea what Biff wanted.

"If I were you, I would run, kid," yelled Eddie, still holding his camera, recording everything.

My heart raced. *This is so wrong. The way they are teasing Marco is not right.*

I knew something should be done. I looked around at the group of boys. *Is it really my job to do something? These are my friends and teammates,*

The Game Changer

and I really want them to keep on liking me. I'm in the "cool" group now, and I want to stay there.

But I couldn't shake the feeling that the way they were treating Marco was wrong. I knew what the right thing was to do, but for some strange reason I stood frozen.

Suddenly Eddie turned and put the camera on me.

"Hey, Tank, what do you think of our new football star? Think there's a spot for him on our team?" asked Eddie.

I did the only thing that came to my mind. I said in an imitation of Marco's accent, "No football, Marco, no football."

Everyone roared with laughter.

Almost everyone.

-5-

As soon as I said those words, I knew I had made a huge mistake. *Giving in to peer pressure and trying to impress people has a weird way of making you say things you don't mean.*

Eddie turned the camera back on Marco. Something bad was about to happen. Holding the football, our new student started to lightly jog toward Biff.

Eddie zoomed in just as Biff rushed toward Marco and hit him. Biff picked him up and slammed him to the ground. The force was so hard that Marco fumbled the football, and his body made a loud smacking sound. His head snapped back, making a harsh cracking sound against the ground.

The Game Changer

Biff had gone too far. In fact, there was no doubt in my mind that what had just happened was wrong and horrible.

I hung my head in shame as the other boys laughed. Eddie ran up and focused the camera on Marco's face as he squirmed to get up.

"What are you boys doing over there?" we heard an adult voice behind us yell. Recognizing Mr. Gomez's voice, everyone scattered. I turned back to see Mr. Gomez helping Marco to his feet and wiping the dirt off his clothes.

Biff walked toward me.

"Tank, wasn't that hilarious?" he asked.

"Yeah, man, so funny," I said in return. I laughed it off, but on the inside I felt terrible. I knew this was another chance to stand up and do the right thing, but I didn't.

The truth was, I was just as bad as Biff and Eddie. I could have stopped their belittling of Marco; I should have done the right thing.

I didn't.

I had seen the wrath of these boys before and

wanted no part of it. Middle school is hard enough without being the center of unwanted attention from Biff and Eddie. So instead of doing what was right, I did what was convenient and cool.

Mr. Gomez walked Marco back into the school as we lined up for stretches. I knew Mr. Gomez would return with Mr. Aarons in a matter of minutes.

We're all going to be in big trouble.

A couple of minutes later, Mr. Gomez returned without saying a word. I kept waiting, but he never mentioned the incident during the rest of the class.

Physical Education was our last class of the day, and football practice was immediately afterward. The schedule worked out perfectly because we were already in the locker room and could dress out for football practice.

I tried to get Marco off my mind once practice started, but I couldn't. *I'm the biggest, strongest kid in the entire school, and when I had the chance to do the right thing, I didn't.*

No one talked about what happened; they all

The Game Changer

seemed to have forgotten. Our first game was only one week away, so we needed to be focused during practice.

After practice, Teddy Nixon, my buddy who played wide receiver, came up to me.

"I can't believe no one got in trouble for the episode before gym class started," he said.

"Yeah, I was waiting for Mr. Aarons to come out to practice and talk to Coach Lawson," I said.

Just then Biff went by laughing.

"What's so funny now?" I asked him, growing tired of his thick, deep laugh.

I was mad at Biff and Eddie, but I was more upset with myself. Even though I hadn't touched Marco, I was just as guilty as the other boys.

"Check your phone, Tank," Biff said as he walked out of the locker room.

I went to my locker and fumbled for my phone. I carried it in the side pocket of my backpack, where the tight fit made it hard to pull out the phone.

As soon as my hand grasped the phone, I knew something was up.

My cell phone was continually buzzing with notifications.

I opened one of the messages and saw that it was a group chat with some of the other boys on the team.

The message read, "Go check *RealTalk*." All the kids at our school used the social media site *RealTalk* to send videos and messages.

I opened up *RealTalk* on my phone and found that Eddie had posted an edited video with music that showed Marco getting bullied by Biff. I could hear my voice on the video; I was laughing loudly. Then the camera zoomed in on me saying, "No football, Marco, no football," in a terrible Spanish accent.

The video had only been posted on the Internet for ten minutes and already had three hundred views.

Oh, no! The clip is going viral!

-6-

I felt deep guilt and regret for not stopping what my teammates had done to Marco that day. I left the locker room with my head hung in disgust.

Glancing back, I could see Eddie walking around, showing everyone the clip on his phone, laughing and enjoying every second of it.

That night I barely slept.

Usually, I would have trouble sleeping because I was so excited to play football. The night before a game, I always tossed and turned with excitement.

This sleeplessness was different.

After eating dinner and doing my homework, I went to bed early, hoping to fall asleep and forget about what had happened that day at school. After a couple hours of not being able to sleep, I reached over and grabbed my phone. I opened up my RealTalk app and couldn't believe my eyes.

The video of Biff bullying Marco now had over 5,000 views with numerous comments. Some responded with laughing emojis, and others made fun of Marco. Several kids left comments on how terribly we had all treated Marco, and I knew they were right.

I slammed down my phone in frustration, filled with regrets.

When given the choice to do what was right or what was convenient, I had made the wrong choice. I made up my mind right then to do something to try to remedy the wrong.

The next morning came much faster than I had hoped. My alarm clock shocked me awake as I wiped the sleep from my eyes.

I felt terrible. I hadn't slept well, and my body was paying for it.

Skipping breakfast is something I never do, but I did that morning. My stomach was already twisting and turn ng; I didn't want to put anything into it to make things worse.

When I got to school, I walked to the cafeteria. I started looking for Marco, but I couldn't find him.

Eddie walked up to me. He was eating an apple and drinking chocolate milk.

"He's not here yet," Eddie said.

"Where is he?" I asked.

"Not sure, everyone is looking for him," he smirked with pieces of apple falling out of the side of his mouth.

I wanted to catch Marco before anyone else so I could apologize to him. Inwardly, I was hoping he had not told Mr. Aarons that I had been a part of what had happened yesterday.

But the video was proof that I was. To be accepted, I had become what I despised—a bully.

The bell rang for our first-hour class and still no sign of Marco.

The students started emptying out of the cafeteria into the main hallway.

A crackling, serious voice came over the loudspeaker as I walked into math class. It was Mr. Aarons.

"Tommy Armstrong, please come to the principal's office," Mr. Aarons said. His voice sounded calm but focused.

All the other kids stopped and stared at me as I took the walk of shame toward the office. I entered and sat down, waiting for Mr. Aaron's door to open.

When it finally opened, I was in complete shock. Two well-dressed people, a man and a woman, left the office. They both carried themselves like important people.

The man walked past me and smiled. "Hola," he said with a grin.

I waved, realizing I had just met Marco's mom and dad for the first time.

This isn't going to be good.

- 7 -

"Come in, Tommy," said Mr. Aarons. Right then, I knew things were not good; Mr. Aarons never called me by my first name.

Everyone called me *Tank*, even Mr. Aarons. The only time anyone ever called me Tommy was when I was in trouble.

I walked in and sat down.

"Tommy, do you know why you are here?" asked Mr. Aarons.

"I think so," I said.

"You think so?" Mr. Aarons repeated with a stern look on his face. He added, "Tommy, please don't make me ask you again."

I nodded. "Yes, sir, I know why I am here," I

mumbled. "I figured Marco would tell you everything, and I was surprised you didn't call me out of practice yesterday," I added.

"Interesting," commented Mr. Aarons.

I paused. *Mr. Aarons can tell I don't know what he means.*

"Tommy, Marco hasn't told me anything," he said.

I was shocked, and my confusion showed.

"You saw his parents—great people, I might add. His dad is well-educated and a very important businessman in Spain. They moved here to launch a new company," said Mr. Aarons.

He added, "In fact, they didn't even mention anything about his first day. They had some questions about our academic programs."

"But surely you know…" I stopped myself.

"Of course, I know! Almost everyone in Union City knows—thanks to that video," said Mr. Aarons.

I was surprised that Marco hadn't reported what happened. Had I been in his place, I would have reported him.

The Game Changer

"Suppose you tell me what happened," encouraged Mr. Aarons.

The time had come to get everything off my chest. Starting from the beginning when Marco was introduced in our math class, I told Mr. Aarons everything—all the way through the incident right before P.E. class.

Mr. Aarons sat and listened. We had a great relationship, and I had let us both down.

When I was finished, Mr. Aarons drew a deep breath before answering. "Tommy, I appreciate your honesty. Truthfully, I am shocked that you were a part of this incident," he said.

His words cut through me like a sharp knife.

"Now what?" I asked.

"Well, Tommy, I will have to decide what happens next. We don't act that way at Union City Middle School, and I know you already know that," he lectured. "We take this kind of behavior really seriously at our school. I will let you know by the end of the day what the consequences will be."

I stood and looked him straight in the eyes.

"Mr. Aarons, I apologize for saying what I said to Marco and for being a part of the bullying," I responded.

Mr. Aarons didn't respond to my apology. His look of disappointment shook me even worse than his words. I had never seen that look from him before.

Not only had I failed to stop the bullies, I had joined in on the bullying.

I had disappointed myself and Mr. Aarons. But telling the truth had lifted a giant burden from my back. Before coming clean to Mr. Aarons, I felt like I had been dropped overboard with a huge weight tied to my back, and I was slowly sinking to the bottom of the ocean.

Even though telling the truth would have consequences, being honest was like cutting away that burden, and I was finally able to breathe again.

Throughout the day, Mr. Aarons used the public address system to call for a number of kids from P.E. class. Toward the end of the day, I heard him call for Biff and Eddie.

The Game Changer

They looked at each other and didn't appear happy. Their video was all the evidence anyone needed to know they had spearheaded the bullying of Marco. I knew I had already mishandled the situation by not stopping them from harassing Marco. I didn't want to make another error in judgment, so I had told the truth.

About ten minutes later, both boys returned to class. They shot me a dirty look. Obviously, they were not happy.

On my way to P.E. class, I stopped in to see Mr. Aarons. Peeking into his office, I saw him working on his computer.

"Sir, have you decided what my punishment will be?" I asked.

Mr. Aarons spun his desk chair toward me.

"Yes, Tommy, due to your actions, you will be suspended for the next two football games," he said.

Suspended? I was going to miss the first two football games of the season!

-8-

In addition to the punishment from the school, I needed to do something else: I had to apologize to Marco.

I didn't see him that day at school. I assumed he was so upset and hurt that he had stayed home from school. That's what I would have done.

At practice, Coach pulled Biff, Eddie, and me to the side. "I am very disappointed in all three of you. Not only have you let me down, but you also let your team down. Now we have to prepare for the next couple of games without you," he said.

I looked at Biff and Eddie, who both glared back at me. But when they turned toward the coach, their expression changed to one of deep sadness.

The Game Changer

Obviously, they didn't feel badly about their actions; instead, they were upset and angry because they had to miss football.

When I got home, I had a long talk with my parents. I told the truth, and so did they. Like my principal and my coach, my parents were disappointed with my poor conduct. As we all sat there together, we shed some tears.

"Tank, you're the biggest kid in the entire school. You know you should never bully someone," my dad reprimanded.

"Dad, I didn't really say anything that bad. The video made me look worse than it was," I said.

"Bullying is one thing; watching someone bully someone else and doing nothing is just as bad!" he said. "You should never have to pull someone else down so you can reach the top."

He was right.

The next morning I waited by the front door of the school. I watched a sleek, black SUV that I had never seen before pulling up, and I knew it had to be Marco.

Lane Walker

When Marco climbed out of the back seat and walked toward the door, I opened it for him. He saw me and took a step back. I could tell he was not quite sure what to think of the situation.

"Hey, Marco, my name is Tank. I just wanted to tell you how sorry I am about what happened yesterday," I said.

I extended my hand, and he reached out and took it. For the first time I was actually eye to eye with Marco. I would have thought he would be nervous, but he wasn't.

I saw confidence in his eyes that I didn't expect—especially after everything that had happened the day before.

"All good," he said with a smile.

We walked down the hallway together, and all eyes were on us. I was twice his size, which must have looked bizarre to everyone.

"You don't have to do this," Marco said.

"Do what?" I asked.

"Walk with me; I'm okay," he said.

His confident tone was convincing. Yesterday's

issue seemingly didn't bother him as much as it had bothered me.

Mr. Aarons stepped out of his office.

"Well, look at this. Two of the biggest football stars in Union City walking down the hallway together," he greeted.

I turned and looked behind me. *Two football stars?* I thought maybe Biff or Eddy was sneaking up behind me, but no one was there.

Marco never broke stride as he waved toward Mr. Aarons and then went straight to his locker. I walked over to Mr. Aarons.

"Mr. Aarons, I don't mean to be rude. Marco seems nice, but if you saw what I saw yesterday in P.E. class, I don't think I would call him a football star. I don't think he's ever played a day of football in his life."

Mr. Aarons started laughing. His laughter wasn't what I call normal; it emanated from deep within him.

"Tank, you still have so much to learn. Not everything is how it seems," he said. "I can tell you for a fact that Marco is one of the best footballers for his age in all of Spain."

Well, Spain must not be too good at football, I thought as I walked away.

-9-

The rest of the school day, my mind raced about Marco. I would catch a glance of him in some of his classes. I saw that he was focused on school. I felt there was something special about him, but what that was, I wasn't quite sure. I had no doubt in my mind that this new mystery kid had something going for himself. If I had gone through what he did yesterday, I would never have come back to Union City Middle School.

But there he was, sitting and listening and even smiling while taking notes in Mr. Simpson's class. Biff's eyes met mine a couple of times. He wasn't smiling. He had received a three-game suspension for his role in the bullying incident.

Instead of feeling bad, it was obvious he blamed Marco. Eddie wasn't quite as angry as Biff, but he also wasn't taking much of the blame and kept making excuses. He had also received a three-game suspension.

This explained why they had glared at me yesterday. I only got a two-game suspension; they each got three. They also knew I had spilled my guts to Mr. Aarons, which isn't the most popular choice among kids my age.

I watched Marco from a distance the entire day. He smiled constantly and never looked sad or worried. My hunch that something was special about Marco was further cemented in my heart. At this point, I couldn't put my finger on what was different about him, but I wanted to know more.

During our fifth-hour social studies class, I leaned over to ask, "Where are you from again?"

"Spain," he said.

"Where in Spain?" I asked.

As he turned to me, his chest lifted in pride, and he said, "Barcelona."

The Game Changer

The way he looked when he said *Barcelona* reminded me of the way Dad had yelled my name after I had hit my first home run.

Then a new thought popped into mind, causing more confusion. So I asked him another question. "Why did you move?"

Marco turned to look at me.

I realized that for the first time he was making eye contact. He looked deeply into my eyes. I noticed his confident spirit shift a little bit.

"My father's job—not my choice," he said.

He didn't need to say anything else. Obviously, the move was hard for him.

I sat in my chair and imagined how hard it would be to move away from my city and my country. I never wanted to move away from Union City. Mr. Aarons had said Marco was one of the best football players in all of Spain. Now he had moved to Union City, and judging by Biff's little episode yesterday, he wouldn't even be able to make our team.

I am a curious person by nature, so my limited

interaction with Marco just filled me with even more questions.

What did his dad do for a job?

How bad was the football in Spain?

When Biff tried to throw him the football, he swatted at it, which looked so awkward. To me, it looked like Marco had never touched a football in his life. Even when he carried the football, he looked awkward and out of place. He held the ball like he was hugging a teddy bear. *No way is this kid good at football.*

As I walked to P.E. class, my mind raced with different ideas and questions. I had to figure out what made Marco so confident.

I dressed and headed outside to the football field. I thought today would be our last class of flag football. I wasn't sure if Mr. Aarons was even going to let us play after the incident that had happened yesterday.

As I approached the field, I could tell something was off. All of my teammates were standing around with a look of annoyance on their faces.

The Game Changer

Mr. Gomez blew his whistle, and we all huddled around him.

As I jogged up, I noticed that he had already divided the class into teams. All my football buddies were wearing a blue schimmel—a solid-colored T-shirt to differentiate between opposing teams. The other half of the class was wearing gold schimmels.

Biff noticed too. I stood next to him as he turned to me, whispering, "We are all on the same team; this is going to be a massacre," he said with a sly grin.

The whistle blew again, this time to signal for all of us to stop talking and to listen. Mr. Gomez walked over and dropped a white and black soccer ball to the ground.

Eddie was the first to respond; he spoke before Mr. Gomez had a chance to say anything.

"I thought we were playing football," he stated sarcastically.

"We are," replied Mr. Gomez with a knowing smile.

- 10 -

"That's a soccer ball," said Biff, who was obviously confused.

"It sure is," said Mr. Gomez. "Did you know that in most countries, other than the United States and Canada, soccer is called football."

"No way! Football is football; and soccer, well, is soccer," jeered Biff.

All the football players stood still—unsure of what to say or do next.

"Actually, what you call football started out in the early 1900s when rugby and soccer were combined and called *gridiron football*. The term *gridiron* was dropped, and the name of the game was shortened to *football*.

The Game Changer

"Americans were the ones who called the game you know and recognize as soccer by that same word. Very few countries took to the name soccer, and to this day, most countries still call the game football," explained Mr. Gomez.

The hair on the back of my neck stood up as I scanned the crowd of students. Marco was standing toward the back, stretching. And he was wearing a blue schimmel, which was the opposite color of the entire football team, including me.

His team consisted of most of the kids who didn't play football—the ones I thought weren't very good athletes.

Soccer was like a foreign language to me. We did have a middle school soccer team, but none of my friends played. Soccer was for the kids who couldn't make the football team…at least that was what I thought.

Our middle school team hadn't won a game in over three years; they were usually the worst team in the league.

We jogged over to the soccer field, which was

located on the other side of the school near the football practice field.

"Do we have to play?" asked one of the football players.

"No, you don't have to, but if you don't, you will receive a zero for the day. Today we are playing a different version of *football*," said Mr. Gomez.

He went over some of the basic rules: no using your hands, offsides, and several more. "We are going to play for twenty minutes," he finished.

Twenty minutes doesn't seem like that long of a game, I thought to myself. *This should be an easy win; we have all the athletes on our team. We have speed and strength; after all, we are top-level, American, middle school football players.*

Everything changed when Mr. Gomez rolled the ball out to the middle of the field and blew the whistle, signaling the start of the game.

The next twenty minutes is hard to describe. One team scored so many goals, Mr. Gomez stopped keeping track when it was 15-0.

Kids were falling down in exhaustion! It seemed

like the longest twenty minutes of my life. I had no idea that the players move constantly in soccer! There are no breaks, and the pace is fast.

When Mr. Gomez blew his whistle ending the game, only six of my team's eleven starting players were left on the field.

Like Biff had predicted, it was a massacre. However, one major part of his prediction was completely wrong. Our team—composed of star football players—didn't win. The other team did—thanks to Marco, who was superhuman on the soccer field!

I have never in my life seen someone so fast, so dominant in a sport. Marco raced around the field and dribbled the soccer ball faster than any of us could run.

He wasn't just fast; he was lightning fast. Seeing Marco on the soccer field was like watching a Broadway play or a sunrise over the mountains.

There was something one of a kind about Marco—something magical.

- 11 -

Our pride was hurt even worse than our tired, aching bodies. We were supposed to be the super athletes—elite football players. The *football* player from Spain made us look silly on the field!

While I was in awe and impressed by Marco's soccer skills, Biff wasn't thrilled. In fact, he was red-faced and angry. He even stomped off the field before the game was over.

Several times Marco made moves on Biff, and twice Biff even fell down and was left watching as Marco raced for a wide-open goal.

Biff didn't like to be shown up, which I thought was kind of confusing, especially after yesterday's episode with Marco.

The Game Changer

If I had to guess, I would say Marco probably scored over twenty goals during that twenty-minute game. Never in my life had I seen one athlete dominate a game like Marco just had. Everything Mr. Aarons had said about Marco's being one of the best "footballers" in Spain now made perfect sense.

Other kids were high fiving him and congratulating him. I walked over and shook his hand. His smile beamed, and I could tell he was at home on the soccer field. He must have missed playing at home in Spain.

Something magical happened to Marco when he stepped on the soccer field. Spain didn't seem as far away; Marco was at home on the green grass. When he played soccer, he was *home*.

As I walked toward him, Tony Smith, one of the boys on our awful soccer team, walked up.

"Marco, you must come out and play on our soccer team," he said.

Marco nodded enthusiastically.

"We practice after school. When gym class is over, if you would like, I will walk with you and introduce you to our coach. I think he will be pretty excited to meet you," said Tony.

As I walked off the field, I overheard Biff talking to Eddie. "That kid thinks he's something special. His time will come, and I will make sure he knows what sport is king around Union City."

"What are you going to do?" asked Eddie.

"I don't know yet, but Marco is going to regret moving to Tennessee," he declared.

I shook my head.

Biff was already serving a three-game suspension for bullying Marco, but he was stubborn. His lack of respect for authority had always been an issue.

"But our soccer team might actually win a game with Marco," Eddie debated.

"Who cares about soccer? No one in Union City does. We are the only winning team around here," argued Biff. "We need to keep it that way. Soccer or "football"—whatever you want to call the game with the white and black ball is stupid and a waste of time."

The Game Changer

After that day, I gained a whole new respect for Marco. It had started with the way he carried himself even after being treated so badly the day before and grew when he smoked my team on the soccer field. He always seemed happy.

I never heard any boasting or saw any hotdogging on the field. He simply played hard and dominated the game. He had world-class speed. In fact, he was the only kid I had ever seen make Eddie look slow.

I got dressed for football practice, and when I hit the practice field, Coach was waiting for me. Biff and Eddie were already standing next to him. "Boys hit the track. You owe me some running," he said.

The three of us ran for the entire hour and a half practice. We had let down Coach and our teammates, and now they had to prepare to play our first two football games without three of their best players.

Our first game against North Central would likely be an easy win. North Central was a basketball-oriented school, and we had beaten them 48-6 last year. Even with our top players absent from the game, we still had too many weapons. But our second game would be against a much tougher team.

Central Middle School in Troy was only a short drive down Highway 51. Their team was recognized as one of the best around, and last year we beat them 21-7. The game had been tough, but without the three of us, it would be even harder this year.

I couldn't do much right now, but I made a promise that I would do everything I could to help my team win, especially after serving my two-game suspension.

Little did I know how that promise would come back to haunt me later.

- 12 -

The Golden Tornadoes' first football game went exactly how I thought it would.

We won the home game against North Central, 24-14. The entire town came out to support us, filling the stadium.

The score would have been better had our kicker, Jimmy Section, not missed all four of the extra points. In his defense, Jimmy wasn't much of a kicker, but he was reasonably good at playing wide receiver and defensive back. Coach really wanted to develop a kicker in case we needed one. During the first football practice, Coach had all of us line up to kick.

Jimmy was one of the only ones who could

make an extra point even once in a while. He was three for ten and won the competition. He hated kicking, and every time he missed, he was so embarrassed. Coach stuck with the kicking plan and kept telling us we would need a kicker at some point in our season.

During the game, the rest of the team wasn't "clicking on all cylinders" and looked sloppy. After the game, Coach told the whole team how the three of us had let them all down. His speech didn't bother me because I knew he was right.

Coach said, "Bad decisions have bad consequences. Those decisions get even worse when you are part of a team!"

He was right. Instead of being a leader, I had been a follower. Instead of standing up and doing what I knew was right, I had taken the cowardly way out.

Biff didn't like how Coach had called him out in front of the team again. He thought the whole incident had been overblown. His parents even went to Mr. Aarons' office and tried to get Biff's suspension lifted. Biff obviously felt no guilt over bullying Marco.

I didn't have to wonder why. What Biff had done to Marco was how he treated many kids. Biff's dad owned the car dealership in town and was known for the same kind of overbearing behavior.

Thankfully, I had only one more game before I could take the field again and do what I loved.

The next day, the school was buzzing about the win the night before. However, the buzz wasn't about the football team's win; rather, the talk was about the soccer team.

Each week the soccer team played the same team the football team did. The soccer team had won its first game in three years, beating North Central 7-1. Marco scored all seven goals.

It didn't bother me that the kids were talking about soccer. I felt good that those players were being recognized for their win.

"They play one game, and people think this kid from Spain is some type of hero or something," Biff muttered to me the next morning.

"Good for them," I said.

"Good for them? Soccer is stupid! Football is king in Union City," declared Biff.

I paused for a second to think because I wanted to make sure of what I was going to say next to Biff. I wasn't going to go along with him anymore. "I think you're looking at it the wrong way. Why can't both sports be popular?"

He turned to stare at me with an aggravated expression. Shaking his head, Biff just walked away.

Clearly, he didn't feel the same way I did. I began to worry about what his next move would be.

The excitement around the game of soccer was small, but there was a growing buzz around town. A good soccer team at Union City Middle School was something new.

Can our town handle two popular fall sports?

- 13 -

The next week of school flew by as we practiced and prepared to take on the Central Middle School Huskies.

Knowing I couldn't suit up for the Central game absolutely destroyed me. I heard they had won their first game 42-0 over Hill County.

Even though I couldn't play, I still owed it to my teammates to be the best practice player I could possibly be. I never took a play off and gave 100 percent the entire practice. Just because I wasn't playing in the game didn't mean I couldn't still help the team get ready.

I was nervous for the Central game. Union City hadn't lost a middle school football game in two years and hadn't lost to Central in four years. I knew they were one of the toughest teams on our schedule, and the game would be on Central's home field.

The winner would be in the driver's seat to win the league championship—something that has become a tradition at Union City. Winning the league championship was a big deal—not just for the team, but for the city as well.

What I found most painful was standing on the sideline, perfectly healthy, dressed in street clothes, and unable to play. Before the game, several of Central's players were laughing and taunting me as I stood on the sideline.

I observed a strange, negative atmosphere during the entire pregame. Our guys seemed out of sync, even a little intimidated, which usually never happens. But normally, the three key players who had been suspended were on the field, making plays.

As soon as the ball was kicked off, I knew we were in trouble.

Central's star running back, Tony Borsick, car-

The Game Changer

ried the opening kickoff back for a touchdown. Then we fumbled our first possession, and the Huskies recovered it.

I watched as Central had their way with our team early. They took full advantage of Biff's, Eddie's, and my own absence from the playing field.

Central led the entire game, but our team made a strong push in the fourth quarter, cutting into the lead, 37-21. However, that was as close as we would get.

When the clock hit :00 in the fourth quarter, Central celebrated. They had ended our four-year winning streak over their school and stopped our undefeated season.

The loss stung even harder for me—mostly because my decision to bully Marco was one of the main reasons we had lost the game.

The bus ride home to Union City was unusually quiet. I can only describe the atmosphere on the bus as depressing. The light drizzle of rain didn't help the situation, leaving a chilly dampness in the air.

When we got back to the school, we slowly unloaded the bus and began carrying all our equipment toward the entrance to the locker room. Entering the school, we heard loud noises already coming from inside. Shocked, we walked in as many of the soccer players were getting ready to leave.

They were celebrating another win, and a win over Central was something to celebrate. Our soccer team hadn't beaten them in so long, no one really knew what the streak was up to. Central had a very good soccer team, but the Golden Tornadoes had pulled out a 4-3 victory!

The mood was mixed as some of the football players congratulated the soccer players. Not everyone shared the soccer team's enthusiasm though. Biff pushed his way through the crowd toward his locker and threw his stuff inside.

Keith, one of the soccer players who rode my school bus, walked past me.

"Good job, Keith! Way to go!" I said, holding up my hand.

The Game Changer

He slapped it with a huge smile on his face. "It was awesome, Tank! Marco scored all four of our goals, and I had two assists," he said.

"Man, it's a team sport, and tonight you guys beat Central!" I said with a smile. Keith walked out with a huge grin. Tonight, he was going home feeling the joy of winning.

The evening was somewhat ironic. The football team had just lost to Central, which meant that we wouldn't have an undefeated season. The loss also meant that we might not be league champs, our biggest goal. And with the soccer team's win, they were the ones in the driver's seat to be league champs.

Growing up, I had always dreamed of being part of Union City sports history…but not this way.

Football practice the next week was just what I needed. My two-game suspension was over, but Biff and Eddie still had one more game left to serve for their involvement. We were playing the Martin Bobcats, and they were no easy team.

I had little interaction with Marco. He was

starting to make some friends on the soccer team. He never sat alone, and all the soccer players idolized him.

No one in Union City had ever seen a soccer player like Marco. Much to his credit, he seemed like the same quiet, new kid who had moved here from Spain a couple of weeks ago.

-14-

The next week things really started to get interesting with Marco. Our history teacher, Mr. Jenkins, had each of us choose a country and prepare a ten-minute presentation to share with the class.

My presentation was on the country of Brazil. I had always been interested in that country after learning my mom's great-grandmother immigrated from there.

Most of the reports were pretty boring, but that all changed when Marco's name was called. He strolled to the front and opened up a PowerPoint with some amazing pictures of Spain.

Even with his strong Spanish accent, Marco spoke with a great sense of pride about his homeland.

He showed a map of Spain with a large star over Barcelona, explaining that his hometown was the most visited city in all of Spain.

He pointed out that the famous artist, Pablo Picasso, lived and studied fine arts in the city. A Picasso museum called Museu Picasso was only a couple of minutes from Marco's house.

Marco was well-prepared and spoke with such passion, sharing facts about the country. I never realized that Barcelona was older than Rome or that it was home to the largest football stadium in Europe. When he said this, my attention narrowed. I realized now that what he called football was actually soccer.

"FC Barcelona is one of the best football clubs in the world," said Marco.

"*Cough*, soccer, *cough*," Biff replied. Some of his cronies laughed loudly, but Biff's comment didn't faze Marco.

"FC Barcelona players are known for their skill and aggressive, attacking brand of football. The club was formed in 1899 and has won thirty Co-

The Game Changer

pas del Rey Trophies, the most prestigious football championship a team can win," said Marco.

Marco further explained that he had played for the FC Barcelona junior league, which had been a great honor. Marco wasn't trying to brag, but obviously, only the elite of the elite soccer players made the club.

His presentation was the best one that day. I was intrigued and impressed with how he expressed his love for Spain and FC Barcelona.

At the end, Mr. Jenkins always let the class ask the presenter a couple of questions. Many hands were raised, and most of the students asked really good questions about living in Spain. Marco told them about tomato bread, cold omelets, and milky coffee. Spain was definitely a different world than the one we knew—and the thought of a cold omelet didn't impress me.

I noticed Mr. Jenkins visually searching the room. I could tell he was trying to find a student who hadn't yet had an opportunity to ask his question.

"Biff, I'm glad to see your hand go up. Go ahead with your question," invited Mr. Jenkins.

I turned to look at Biff, afraid of what he was going to say. Marco stayed calm and cool, unaffected by the thought of what Biff was going to ask.

"So, do they have *real* football there?" Biff asked.

At first, it seemed like Biff was genuinely interested in knowing if they had real tackle football in Spain.

"Real football?" Marco asked puzzled.

"Yeah, you know, like we have here in the United States. The kind of football where players hit each other, and people like to watch the action. You know, *real* football. We all know that no one really cares about soccer," said Biff.

"Okay, okay," Marco said. "I see your question. Here is one last picture of the most recent game I attended in Barcelona."

Marco was prepared for Biff's sarcastic question!

A PowerPoint picture of a sports stadium with thousands of people filled the screen. In the pic-

The Game Changer

ture, Marco was surrounded by people, most of them sporting FC Barcelona jerseys.

The entire class went quiet at the sight of so many people in a packed stadium. The picture obviously showed how huge soccer was in Spain.

"Wow! Marco, that had to be a great experience! Do you happen to know how many people attended that game?" asked Mr. Jenkins.

"Around 100,000 people were there that day," said Marco proudly.

I guess soccer or football, or whatever it is called in Spain, is an extremely popular sport. I had never seen a picture with so many people in it.

Neither had Biff. He mumbled something unintelligible and sat down.

- 15 -

At practice, Biff didn't even try to hide his feelings. "I can't stand the soccer kid," he said, turning to Eddie.

"Yeah, he thinks he's so cool," said Eddie, jumping on the Biff bandwagon.

"No one around here cares about stupid soccer," said Biff.

I turned to face them. "What's your real problem with Marco?" I asked.

Shocked, Biff turned to stare at me.

"Well, look who was impressed with some picture of a bunch of people watching players kick a ball down the field," Biff said sarcastically.

"I thought it was interesting," I replied. Then I

The Game Changer

added, "So what's your issue with Marco anyway? You've had a problem with him since the moment he moved here."

"I'll tell you what the problem is," Biff said as he walked toward me. "Some new rich kid moves into our town, gets us all in trouble for having a little fun, and now he tries to make soccer more popular than football. I don't see how you can like him, Tank," said Biff.

The way Biff talked about Marco made me think he was angry at him for no good reason. He just wanted to feel like he was better than Marco.

"If the kid likes soccer, so what? He seems nice," I said.

Biff turned and looked at Eddie. "Looks like Tank is soft for the soccer star. Let me guess, you guys are buddies now?" he said.

"Maybe, I don't know. He seems cool to me," I said.

"Oh, does he? And this is coming from the captain of our football team? Have you already forgotten that you haven't played this year because of him? Our undefeated record is broken while the Huskies of Central are celebrating our defeat," he sneered.

Obviously, Biff blamed Marco for the three of us getting into trouble. He even blamed him for the football team's loss to Central. He couldn't see himself as the problem—only Marco. Biff had taken absolutely no accountability for his behavior, and Marco was an easy scapegoat.

I shook my head and walked away. Biff will have to learn that lesson the hard way.

Just as I was about to sit down on the bench to tie my football cleats, I saw Eddie and Biff walking toward me.

"One more thing you need to remember, Tank. We are your friends and your teammates," said Biff. "Don't forget that if the time ever comes again when you need to make a decision, you better choose your football brothers."

With that ultimatum, I knew right away what Biff was upset about. Not only did he blame Marco for his troubles, but he also blamed me. He felt that

The Game Changer

I had ratted him out when I told Mr. Aarons the truth about all of us hassling Marco.

"Yeah, remember, Tank, we are the ones playing *real* football. We have since the fifth grade, and some new kid can't change that," barked Eddie, feeding off Biff's anger.

This wasn't the time or the place for this discussion, and I could tell our conversation wasn't going well. But I had to get ready. We had a game to win on Thursday, and I didn't have time to waste on two guys who couldn't even play. I kept lacing up my cleats, ignoring the two boys standing next to me.

After a couple seconds of silence, they turned and walked away. They finally got the hint that I was done wasting my time with them for today. Just when I thought they were finally gone, Biff stopped and turned back toward me.

"Tank!" he said in a loud voice that surprised me.

I stopped tying my laces and looked up.

"Be careful," he warned. "Don't get too friendly

with the soccer star. I can already picture you running around on the soccer field."

"Yeah, don't forget you are a *football* player. Don't go and make a soccer switch on us," said Eddie, laughing.

-16-

The week was filled with anticipation. After a tough loss to Central, our whole team was ready to get back on the field and show everyone that we were still a great team. I couldn't wait to play.

On Wednesday nights, our team enjoyed dinner together after practice. The day before the game was always exciting, and our parents loved organizing a team meal.

I was halfway through my second plate of spaghetti when Jeff Nicolson sat down next to me. Jeff was a good friend and currently our starting quarterback. He wasn't as good as Eddie on the football field, but he was a far nicer guy.

"How you feeling, Tank?" Jeff asked.

"Good! I'm ready to play, and I can't wait to get back on the field," I said. The two-game suspension had given me extra time to reflect on how much I loved football. One of the two places I felt completely at home was between the marks on the football field.

"I am glad you're back; I need you to protect me," Jeff said with a laugh.

I took great pride in protecting our quarterback and not letting any defenders slip past me. Being big helped, but in football, a lineman must be strong and quick. Not only did I have the size, but I also had great hands and moved my feet well.

Watching Jeff get hit so many times against Central had been hard on me.

"What are you doing tonight?" asked Jeff.

"I have some history homework from Mr. Jenkins. After I finish, I'll probably just chill the rest of the night and go to bed early," I said.

He nodded, but I could tell he wanted to ask me something. "Why? What are you doing?" I asked.

The Game Changer

I thought maybe he wanted to play video games or come over to hang out.

"I think I'm going to the soccer game. It's at home, and I want to see the new kid play," said Jeff. "After watching Marco's presentation, I kind of want to see what soccer is all about. I've never watched a game, but it seems to be pretty popular in Spain."

"For sure," I said.

I kept eating my spaghetti as my mind flashed back to the picture of Marco standing in the packed stadium.

"I think I'll go with you," I said.

I finished my meal and talked to my parents about the soccer game that started at six o'clock. It was already 5:30, so Jeff and I headed toward the soccer field where Union City was warming up.

The soccer schedule was quite different. The team's first two games were on a Thursday, the same night as our football games. But tonight's game was on Wednesday. Their opponent, Jefferson, was really good. I overheard some of the soccer players earlier telling Mr. Aarons that Jefferson was undefeated.

This game would be an early battle of two undefeated teams. The soccer team had been extremely excited the entire day at school. They wore their soccer jerseys with pride and were walking the halls differently since Marco had arrived.

Bright lights surrounded the field as Jeff and I took a seat in the bleachers. The crowd started to grow as parents and spectators piled into the aluminum stands.

I noticed that some of our other football teammates had joined us. I guess they also wanted to see the big soccer game. I had no idea about the rules or how the game was played, but I knew three facts about the game. Soccer was a fast-moving physical sport. Those playing forward, midfielder, and defender couldn't touch the soccer ball with their hands. The goalkeeper or "goalie" was the only one who could catch the ball legally and use his hands.

That was the sum total of what I knew about

The Game Changer

the game of soccer. At this point in my life, that was all I cared to know. But after watching and listening to Marco, I was becoming more interested in the game he loved so much.

The horn blew loudly signaling warm-ups were over, and the game was about to start. Both teams paused and lined up as the national anthem blared over the speakers.

Soccer had slowly gained in popularity in the hallways at school. Winning helped, and Marco was the reason for the wins. Now Union City citizens were showing up to see Marco display his talent on the soccer field.

I thought having two good teams—football and soccer—was great because it made people talk more about Union City in general. I was impressed with the turnout. In fact, people were standing around the field as well because the stands were so crowded.

I looked toward the net our goalie was guarding. I squinted and couldn't believe my eyes. Standing behind the goalie were Biff and Eddie. I was shocked that the pair of troublemakers had come to watch the soccer game.

Maybe Marco's presentation had prompted them to be interested in soccer too...*or maybe they were here for another reason...*

- 17 -

The game with Jefferson was fast-paced and entertaining. Even though I didn't know much about the sport, I could tell this was a game between two good teams.

Marco was by far the best player on the field. Jefferson had better players overall, but we had the best one. Marco could do it all. He did things with the soccer ball I didn't even know were possible.

Our middle school soccer team played two 20-minute halves. Thanks to two goals by Marco in the first half, we were leading Jefferson 2-1.

I was starting to realize why Marco was so capable of moving at high speeds. Soccer is a game that doesn't stop! Besides an occasional time-out or injury, the game is fast-paced and constantly in motion.

During halftime, Jeff and I walked toward the concession stand. I loved popcorn, especially when watching sports.

We were standing in line when I felt a nudge at my back. I turned to see Biff and Eddie.

"What's up, *ladies?*" Biff asked with a laugh.

I rolled my eyes. *Dealing with Biff and Eddie was just what I didn't need.*

"What's up?" I asked.

"Oh, nothing, just taking in this soccer stuff. Pretty boring if you ask me," said Biff.

"Yeah, seems like a stupid sport," added Eddie as he looked toward Biff for approval. Eddie was such a follower; he was always trying to impress Biff. I noticed that the more Eddie tried to awe Biff, the meaner Biff was to him.

Biff treated me differently. Though he could be annoying and pick at me, he knew not to take his heckling too far.

"I'm enjoying it," I said firmly.

The Game Changer

"You would, Tank. Imagine your big body running around, trying to kick that little black and white ball. Now that would be a sight I would pay to watch," he said.

Eddie started laughing until I shot him a look.

"What do you want, Biff?" I asked.

"I just want to have a little fun! Lighten up, man," he said.

"Fun? I don't think that is what you want at all. Isn't that the reason you are still missing another football game?" I asked.

Eddie stepped back, staring at me. I could tell he wasn't used to someone standing up to Biff.

Biff looked at me, and for a second, I thought he was going to push me.

"Relax, Tank. I was only having some fun. Come on, Eddie, these two guys are serious soccer fans now. Let them enjoy the rest of the game," said Biff.

"Thanks, I think that's a good idea," I said, staring deep into Biff's eyes. I wanted him to know I was tired of his aggravation and not afraid of him.

Biff took a big step back and turned. I watched as the pair walked back toward the soccer field.

"Maybe those knuckleheads will go home," said Jeff, whispering so only I could hear him.

"I could only wish," I said, as I turned back to order my popcorn. It was obvious from Biff's attitude that he hadn't learned anything from his punishment.

I knew my wishful thinking wasn't going to be enough. My mind raced, trying to understand why Biff is always harassing people. He seemingly lived to make other people feel bad about themselves.

Jeff and I walked back and joined our friends in the student section. The crowd roared as the Golden Tornadoes jogged back onto the field.

The cheers gave me goosebumps. The crowd was into the game, and so was I. I thought I was only attending to watch a soccer game, but as it turned out, I was fascinated by the sport.

The horn sounded, signaling the end of halftime and the start of the second and final half. The second half started with a quick goal by Marco.

The Game Changer

I had never seen such a fantastic play. Someone had kicked the ball up to midfield, and out of nowhere, Marco streaked ahead, tipping the ball. He outran all the defenders, streaking toward the goal and faking a kick. The goalie was jumping all around—not sure of Marco's next move.

Suddenly Marco kicked the ball into the air, jumped high, setting up a perfect header to slam the ball into the net for a goal.

Our team took a 3-1 lead!

The game went back and forth, and with three minutes left, a player from Jefferson scored a goal, making the game 3-2. We still had the lead, but Jefferson quickly scored another goal, tying the game with 1:35 left.

How was it that they did not score a single goal in the entire half, then scored two goals in less than a minute? Something doesn't make sense.

It was dark, but I squinted toward our goalie, trying to see if anything was out of place. In the dark behind the goalie net, I saw two figures.

-18-

For some reason, our goalie kept looking behind him toward the two figures. Something inside my brain clicked, and I knew what was happening. I jumped up from my seat and ran down the bleachers. I looked toward the scoreboard on my way, watching as the clock kept ticking down. I glanced up one more time and saw that we had only thirty seconds on the clock.

As I rounded the corner toward the goalie, a Jefferson player came streaking toward the net. The play was now one on one—just him and the goalie.

I didn't make it in time.

The Jefferson player made a quick move, and

The Game Changer

our goalie dove late as the soccer ball hit the back of the net. The horn sounded, signaling a 4-3 win for Jefferson.

Our soccer team had lost its first game and maybe a shot at winning the league title. I was winded by the time I made it to the spot where I had seen the figures behind the goalie.

"What are you doing?" I asked.

"What? Us?" Biff said as innocently as possible.

When I turned around, I watched as huge tears welled up in our goalie's eyes. Chris was upset... and not because the team had lost.

Chris glared in our direction. Teammates came toward him and helped him up. They walked toward the sideline in disappointment.

"I know what you did," I said to Biff and Eddie. "I could see you yelling stuff toward Chris. Why would you do that?" I asked in disbelief. "These are our friends—our classmates."

I could tell Eddie was starting to feel bad. He backed away, drifting slowly toward the darkness behind the goalie.

"I'm sorry, Tank," Eddie said as he stepped into the shadows.

Now it was just Biff and me.

"What's your problem?" Biff asked.

"My problem?" I asked.

"It's just a stupid soccer game," snarled Biff.

"Maybe to you…" I could feel the anger inside starting to push up through my stomach toward my throat. Biff and I were now face to face, with only a couple of inches separating us. Biff's stare shifted, and he dropped his eyes at the realization of just how angry I was.

"Football is king in Union City, Tank. Don't you ever forget that," Biff warned.

"Are you seriously jealous of people liking soccer?" I asked.

"I'm not jealous of anything," Biff said.

"Yes, you are! You're jealous of the soccer team and of Marco."

That comment got Biff's attention. He didn't like what I had said; the dark look on his face made it obvious.

The Game Changer

This wasn't just about the sport of soccer. Biff was jealous of Marco and the attention that soccer was getting because of Marco's ability.

Biff and Eddie's badgering of Chris had helped Jefferson beat us. What they had done was shameful.

Suddenly, Mr. Aarons stepped between us. I hadn't noticed, but a large group of kids had circled around, anticipating a fight. If Mr. Aarons hadn't arrived when he did, a fight might have broken out. I was certainly furious enough to do it.

Even as Mr. Aarons separated the two of us, I never took my eyes off Biff, shooting him a sharp glare.

Looking back, I'm glad Mr. Aarons showed up because a fight would have just made everything worse.

When he finally walked away from the field, he turned in my direction. "Remember you're a football player—just like us," said Biff.

I was nothing like them, and I never would be.

-19-

My heart broke for Marco and our soccer team. They had been in a position to beat our rivals and possibly win a league title.

Union City had started a soccer team twenty years ago, but the team had never won a league title.

Knowing that Biff and Eddie had initially positioned themselves behind Chris in order to distract him, made this loss sting even worse.

Our football game against Jefferson was tomorrow, but my mind was on Marco and his team. I had known Biff and Eddie were up to no good, and I felt guilty for not stopping them in time.

The next day in school, everyone was talking

The Game Changer

about the soccer game. I went up to Marco, who was now very popular, as he stood in the middle of his soccer teammates.

To my surprise, Marco was still smiling. I wouldn't have been able to handle a loss that well if what had happened to him had happened to me.

"I wanted to let you know I'm sorry," I said. The crowd of boys stopped talking and separated.

"No problem, Tank," said Marco.

"Yes, it is a problem. You lost your chance at a league championship because of what happened. It's not fair. I just wanted to let you know that a lot of guys on the football team support you guys," I said.

"Thank you, but we still have a chance to win the league championship," he said.

"Still win the league championship—after losing a league game?" I questioned.

"Yes, at least that is what Jeff told me," replied Marco.

I turned toward Jeff.

He was already answering my question before I could ask.

"If we win the rest of our games and someone beats Jefferson, we would be co-champs," explained Jeff.

Marco nodded, "We will play well and win the rest." His tone was confident—not cocky.

"I know you were cheering for us," said Marco.

"Good, because we were. I think it's awful what Biff and Eddie did," I said.

"I know. Remember one bad apple doesn't spoil the orchard," he said.

I walked away, wishing there was more I could do to show support for the soccer team. I left the cafeteria and shifted my thinking toward our football game against Jefferson. Playing well tonight was important. I owed it to my team. Plus, winning without Biff and Eddie would hopefully show them that the team was bigger than any individual.

Jefferson has always had a great football team, and in a way, our soccer team had a lot in common with our football team. Both of our teams had to win the rest of our games and hope someone else beats the team to whom we had lost a game. Being

The Game Changer

co-champions was better than not being champions at all.

One huge problem was standing in the way of both teams. We hadn't played the best team in our conference yet. The Hickman Hoosiers were still on the schedule, and Hickman was our biggest rival and strongest opponent.

Last year we had beaten them on the last play of the game by one point. But Hickman's soccer team has won the league championship for five consecutive years, including a 7-1 beatdown of our soccer team on the way to the championship last year.

But now wasn't the time to worry about Hickman or Biff. I had to focus on Jefferson. If we lost again, our shot at the league title would be gone.

-20-

Union City fans usually filled the bleachers for every game, but I was a little worried that our loss last week would affect the turnout. It didn't.

During warm-ups, I was both anxious and nervous. I didn't want people to think I was just bigger than everyone, I wanted to prove to everyone that I was a great football player.

In a strange way, sitting out the Central game had been good for me. Watching my team play, seeing them battle and give everything they had against Central had motivated me. I had something to prove.

I planned on blocking and driving whoever lined up against me into the ground. That was my job as the anchor on both the offensive and defensive line.

Minutes before the game, I scanned our bleachers, and to my surprise, the entire soccer team was in the stands. They were cheering and supporting us—even after last night's loss.

My heart filled with Golden Tornado pride. As I walked over to the bench to get a drink, I noticed Biff and Eddie in street clothes on the sideline. I hadn't seen them since last night. I was pretty sure they had skipped school today. I was still angry about last night and planned to do everything I could to avoid both of them.

They didn't look in my direction; they were trying to avoid me too. Biff wasn't used to anyone's standing up to him, so he was still in shock from last night. Seeing me actually angry can have that effect on people.

I was still disappointed in myself for not noticing that they were heckling our goalie until it was too late. I should have helped sooner. Our soccer team deserved to win that game and the league title. And a win over Hickman would be nearly impossible.

A battle between two good football teams, this game was going to be entertaining. I wasn't going to let us lose. We couldn't let Jefferson knock us out of the race for a share of the league championship.

From the opening kick-off to the final horn, we dominated. The game was so much easier now that I was an eighth grader. I felt stronger and faster, and on the field, I bullied people around. At times I drove two Jefferson defenders into the ground at the same time. Our running backs ran wild through the holes I opened.

Jefferson didn't know who, or what, hit them. By the time they got their bearings back, the game was over, and we had won 48-14. The highlights featured several long runs, as well as lengthy touchdown passes. Our only negative was our kicker. Jimmy missed two extra points at the beginning of the game, so Coach stopped trying to kick and decided to go for a two-point conversion every time we scored a touchdown.

The Game Changer

A bunch of fans waited to congratulate us as we walked off the field to the locker room. A group of soccer players was waiting by the fence.

"Hey, Tank, good job!" yelled Marco.

"Thank you! We appreciate you guys cheering us on!" I yelled back.

I walked toward them and gave each of them a fist bump.

"You move well for a big guy; you have good feet and quick hands," said Marco.

"I'll take that as a compliment coming from you," I said with a smile. I had never seen another person on this earth who moved like Marco did on a soccer field.

I said my goodbyes before jogging into the locker room. The atmosphere was rowdy and full of positive energy. When I walked in, some of the seventh-grade guys ran up to me cheering loudly. I smiled and walked toward my locker.

All the cheering stopped so suddenly I was caught off guard. I turned back toward the guys to see what had happened. Biff was standing there with Eddie hiding in his shadow. Biff's presence had instantly sucked the positivity out of the locker room as he just stood there staring at everyone.

After a couple of awkward minutes, he spoke. "We got nothing to cheer about. So what if we won? If we don't win every game, then this game won't matter. Lucky for you guys, I will be back next week," he said.

Then he turned and looked directly toward me. "Nothing or no one will stop me from playing this time," he said.

His presence was like a huge vacuum sucking all the happiness out of every soul in that locker room. Yes, Biff and Eddie were great players, and we needed them to win the rest of our games, but I wish Biff could realize what a negative impact his attitude could have. We wouldn't beat Hickman without both of them. Even with their playing, beating the Hoosiers was going to be a tough task.

Somehow, I had to figure out a way to get along

The Game Changer

with both of them; we were teammates. But so much had already changed this year.

Little did I know bigger changes were on the way...

-21-

The night before the Martin football game, Marco and the soccer team won 3-2 over the Bobcats. The game was exciting, but I wanted to attend the games because Marco was my friend.

I now understood much more about the strategy and skill level needed to play soccer. Soccer, or *football* as Marco called it, was an intense sport that required hard work and endurance. Now I not only respected but also thoroughly enjoyed the sport of soccer.

The Martin football game was much tougher than I thought it would be. Maybe that's because we were looking forward to next week's matchup against Hickman instead of concentrating on the game at hand. Or maybe we had become overconfident and lost our focus.

Whatever the issue was, it wasn't good, and our shortcomings showed on the football field. Martin was a team we should have easily beaten by three or four touchdowns. Instead, we found ourselves in a tight battle on our home field.

The football game went back and forth, with neither team quitting. Every time we would score and take the lead, Martin struck back. They were quick and well-coached. The Bobcats weren't intimidated even when they came into Union City to play against us.

In the fourth quarter, the game was tied 21-21, and Martin had the ball. Biff made a great tackle on their quarterback, stripping the ball from him, while Eddie recovered on the Bobcat 20-yard line.

Coach Carter called three run plays to the right, directly over my side of the line as we punched the ball down to the Bobcat three-yard line.

Martin called a time-out on first and goal with forty-five seconds left. If we were to score, the game would pretty much be over. The raucous home crowd grew quiet as Eddie lined up to take the snap. He turned and handed the ball off to Biff on the right side, directly behind me.

I stayed low and pushed with all my might as three Bobcat defenders smashed into me on the goal line with a loud collision. I heard a roar from the crowd as I hit the ground. Rolling over to my side, I saw the referee hold up his hands signaling a touchdown.

The Golden Tornadoes had a six-point lead as Jimmy trotted onto the field to kick the extra point. The snap was good; the holder squeezed the ball and spun it so the laces faced out.

Jimmy missed the extra point.

An eerie silence fell over the crowd. If Martin scored and kicked the extra point, we would lose—not only the game, but also our hopes of being league champs.

Coach called a time out. I took a drink of water and glanced at the clock. Martin had the football and forty seconds left to win the game.

The Game Changer

Jimmy kicked off and sent the ball deep into our territory. We tackled the Bobcat runner on our thirty-five-yard line.

They couldn't possibly go sixty-five yards in that short time, could they?

In the defensive huddle, I could tell some of the guys were scared we were going to lose.

"Focus, Tornadoes! Stop staring around with those big eyes. Do your job, and we win," I yelled in the huddle.

"Yeah, listen to Tank. We got this!" echoed Biff.

His timely support surprised and motivated me at the same time. The others felt it too. Biff's added encouragement was just what we needed.

We sprinted up to the line. The Martin center snapped the football to the quarterback, and I raced toward him. As he dropped back to pass, I spun off the offensive lineman and hurtled my body toward him.

Just as he was about to throw a pass, my collision caused him to drop the ball.

"FUMBLE!" I yelled, diving toward the ball.

My right hand made contact, sending the ball flying farther into the backfield.

I looked up to see Biff jumping on it, recovering the fumble. The ball was ours, and the football game was officially over. I ran toward Biff. The defense jumped up and down and grabbed Biff in excitement.

In the chaos, our eyes met. Biff leaned in so only I could hear him. In a seriously dark tone, he said, "This doesn't change anything between us, Tank."

I guess he's still angry about the incident at the soccer field.

Even the thrill of victory had been unable to heal that wound.

-22-

Most of our home crowd ran onto the field to celebrate with us. We now had what we had hoped for—a chance to beat Hickman—and at least attain a tie for the league championship.

"Big hit, Tank! Big hit!" yelled Marco, giving me a high five. Marco was starting to love our version of football—American football.

The rush of a big victory felt great, but that feeling was dampened, knowing that Biff still had issues with me. Even in our greatest moment as teammates, he hadn't forgotten about our past problems.

I enjoyed the victory, but if we didn't beat Hickman, then we would still fall short of our goals.

"Gather around, boys," Coach said in the locker room.

"I just got a call with some good news: Hickman beat Central 21-14 tonight. Beating Hickman next week means there will be a three-way tie for the league championship. We still have a chance."

We still have a chance. Hickman was undefeated. They had beaten Central, who had beaten us. If we could beat Hickman, we would have a share of the title.

Hickman was a great team, and I knew we couldn't make any mistakes if we wanted to beat them. We needed to win so we wouldn't lose our streak of league championships. In so doing, the strong Union City football tradition would be preserved.

I packed up all my things in a rush to meet Marco and the others at Antonio's Pizza Palace to celebrate the win. Antonio's has great food, but an even better arcade where we all love to spend our allowances.

Marco loved the claw machine game. He was

The Game Changer

fantastic at it and usually left with several stuffed animals every time we frequented the arcade.

Bending down to tie my shoes, I had a strange feeling. I scanned the locker room, looking for Biff, and spotted him on the other side of the room. I could hear him replaying the final moments of the game with Eddie. Biff always loved to play the role of a hero, and his fumble recovery had put a big spotlight on him tonight.

I was just glad we had won the game and still had a chance at the league title. I closed my locker and headed toward the exit door.

As I was leaving, Coach Carter motioned for me to come into his office. My first thought was that I was in trouble. Usually, Coach didn't bring a player into his office unless he had something to discuss with him. I tried to read his body language, but it was hard to tell if he was happy or upset.

Coach Green, our special teams coach, was also waiting in the office.

I shyly opened the door, closing it behind me. "Did you want me, Coach?" I asked sincerely.

"Yeah, Tank. Come on in. I do have something or someone I want to talk to you about," said Coach Carter. "Coach Green and I have been talking. We both know there were some issues at the beginning of the season, and…"

Before Coach could say another word, I interrupted him. "Things are fine with Biff and me," I reassured him. I knew he had seen the tension on the field and had no doubt heard about our near fight at the soccer game. *Coach wants to make sure all our heads are in the game with Hickman coming to Union City next week.*

"Tank, this isn't about Biff," said Coach Carter. I stood stunned.

"Well, who is this about?" I asked.

"That new soccer player," said Coach Green.

"Marco? What about him?" I asked. "Whatever Biff told you is a lie. Marco is a great kid. He has been nothing but nice to Biff…to all of us," I said.

This time I was going to defend Marco and do the right thing. He had become a great friend— one that I trusted.

The Game Changer

"Biff didn't say anything bad about the kid," said Coach Green.

"Coach, now I'm confused. What do you want to talk about Marco for?" I asked.

"I am going to be straight with you, Tank. Hickman is good. No, they are great," he said.

I nodded. *I already knew that.*

"I need you to talk to your buddy, Marco," he said.

"Talk to him about what?" I asked one more time, still not getting what he was hinting at.

"Talk him into playing football with us," urged Coach Carter.

"Wait, say that again," I said.

"Tank, we need Marco for the Hickman game. I'm afraid if he doesn't play, we will lose that game," he said.

Marco playing football? He has never played American football, and the only time I ever saw him hold a football didn't end well. I was not convinced this idea would end well either.

-23-

"Coach, Marco isn't a football player...I mean like *our* football," I said.

Coach Carter took a deep breath and looked at Coach Green.

"Tank, the kid has a golden leg, and we need a kicker badly," said Coach Green.

What Coach was getting at finally hit me. *He wants Marco to be our kicker.* Jimmy had already missed so many kicks this year, and his misses had almost cost us another game today.

"You want me to ask Marco to put on the pads and play football this week—to play against the best team we have played all year?" I asked in shock.

The Game Changer

"Yes, that is exactly what we want you to do," he said.

"I was at his game yesterday, Tank. I have never seen a kid kick a ball like that. Not even high school kids can kick like Marco. He would be a huge asset for us against Hickman," said Coach Carter.

I slumped in the chair. *Everything they're saying makes perfect sense, and I feel silly that I haven't thought of it. A key player has been sitting with me every day at lunch, and the thought has never crossed my mind to talk to him about playing American football.*

Then another thought hit me—although this wasn't a good one. I leaned forward with a serious look. "Does Biff know about this?" I asked.

Coach Carter leaned back in his chair and chuckled. "That's the craziest thing, Tank. It was Biff's idea," he said.

What? Biff's idea to have Marco join the team?

"Really?" I was so stunned by Coach Carter's answer, I couldn't think of anything to say. Both coaches could tell I was as bewildered as they were.

"He came to us this morning and said he had an idea that would help our team win, and that idea was having Marco join the team as our kicker," said Coach Carter.

The whole idea made sense; I simply couldn't believe Biff had suggested it. I thought about the proposal a little longer and said, "I guess I can talk to him."

Then I added, "Maybe Biff and I can both go talk to him. That might help with everything else that happened."

Playing football together could be the perfect bridge to dispel the anger and envy that Biff felt toward Marco. I had no idea whether Marco would want to meet with Biff after what Biff had done.

"One more thing, Tank. Biff thought of the idea, but he made it very clear that he wouldn't be apologizing or begging Marco to play. In fact, he said he doesn't want to talk to him at all. But knowing Marco could help us win the championship made Biff want him on the team," explained Coach Carter.

The Game Changer

So Biff won't talk to him or apologize but wants him to play?

"Seems like an awkward situation to me. But I agree, we need Marco against Hickman," I said. It was apparent Coach felt bad about asking me to talk to Marco after Biff's abrupt words.

"So you will talk to him?" asked Coach Green.

"I will talk to him; at least I will throw out the idea," I said.

"Great! Good luck, Tank," said Coach Green.

I walked to the exit door and left the locker room. Antonio's was only a couple of blocks away from the school. On the walk to the pizzeria, I rehearsed how I would ask Marco to play.

What will he say? Will our friendship be hurt if he says no?

My stomach twisted as I opened the door to the arcade. When our crew spotted me, Marco waved and motioned me over to a table.

I guess now is as good a time as ever, I thought as I sat down next to him.

-24-

Antonio's was loud with the sound of music and kids having a good time. The arcade machines boomed loud theme music, and the irresistible smell of bread and cheese filled the air.

"Jimmy broke your record in *Alien Attack III*. He hit a huge combo on his last life," Marco said.

"Oh, man, I thought that record would never be broken," I said.

"Records are always meant to be broken," Marco replied with a smile.

"And that last play was awesome. The quarterback didn't know what hit him. He probably thought you were a semitruck or something comparable," Marco joked.

The Game Changer

"It felt good," I said, recognizing my chance. "About the game, are you starting to like football?" I asked.

Marco looked surprised. "Like football? I have always loved football. You know that, Tank," he said. I laughed, knowing he was teasing me about the two different games we called "football."

"But, yes, I do like *American* football. Very fun to watch, but I definitely like my 'football' better," said Marco.

Is that a hint? Does he mean he would never want to play American football? A million questions were running through my mind. I searched for a way to ask him without making it sound awkward.

"Why?" he asked. Marco knew me well enough to know that something was on my mind. He must have realized I had something else I wanted to say.

"Like…would you ever want to try it…like play American football?" I asked.

"Like wear a helmet and have Biff McGraw destroy me again? I don't think that sounds like fun," he said, laughing.

When I didn't respond with laughter, he could tell I was serious.

"Tank, why would you want me to play your football?" asked Marco.

"We need you and your strong legs. If we don't have a kicker against Hickman, we are in big trouble." *There, I said it.*

"A kicker? Like all I would have to do is kick the ball? No one will try to rip me in half?" asked Marco.

"Just kick. Yes, they will try to hit you, but I promise no one will touch you. I'll make sure of that," I promised.

I was surprised when Marco went quiet. I could tell he was actually considering the idea.

"I want to help you and your team, but I don't know if this is a good idea, Tank."

"I understand. Don't do it just because we are friends. You will still be my friend—even if you don't want to play," I said.

"Let me think about it. Let's forget about it for now and go play some air hockey," he said.

The Game Changer

"Sounds good to me—unless you are afraid to lose again," I said as we darted toward the air hockey table in the corner of the game room.

The rest of the night we had a blast. We ate pizza, played games, and had so much fun that I almost forgot about our conversation.

Our parents were picking us up at nine o'clock since we had school the next day. Mom let me stay out a little later than my usual, earlier curfew because she knew we were celebrating a big win, and tomorrow was Friday.

I saw her black SUV pull up at almost nine o'clock. Grabbing my jacket, I said goodbye to our crew. I was walking out when I felt a hand grab my shoulder. I turned and saw it was Marco.

"I have thought about it; I will do it. I will play and kick your American football," he said.

"Awesome! Thank you!" I said, smiling from ear to ear.

I turned to leave when Marco spoke up.

"Just one thing, Tank. I want Biff to ask me to play. If he asks me, I will play," said Marco.

"You want Biff to ask you to be on the team?" I repeated.

"Yes, that is my only condition," he said.

As I jumped into Mom's car, my mind raced. I had known Biff for a long time, and there was no way he was going to ask Marco to play.

All I can do is try.

-25-

That night I wrestled with ideas and ways to convince Biff he needed to be the one to ask Marco. Finally, I decided to just be honest and tell him Marco wouldn't play if he didn't ask him personally. Honesty was always the best policy, and the rest would fall on Biff's shoulders.

The next morning, I walked into school on a mission. I looked all over for Biff but couldn't find him. Finally, a couple minutes before the first hour bell rang, Biff slipped into the cafeteria for breakfast.

I waited for him to grab his plate and watched as he sat down to eat. I walked over and motioned for Eddie to slide over, which he did instantly.

"I talked to Coach," I said.

"Yeah and…?" Biff said. He instantly put on his tough front to impress Eddie. I had watched him switch his personality hundreds of times. By now I was used to how he changed according to his mood.

I leaned closer so he could hear me. "That was a good idea," I said.

"What was?" Biff said, trying to act like he didn't know what I was talking about.

"Eddie, go get me another milk," he ordered. Eddie immediately jumped up and left the table.

"What's your point?" asked Biff.

"He said he would play," I said.

Biff nodded, happy to hear that Marco had agreed to play.

"It's what's best for our team…we need to win that game," Biff said.

"I agree," I said.

I quickly added, "He made just one small request. He will join the team only if you ask him to play."

The Game Changer

"What? Are you serious?" he asked. Eddie had just returned with his milk, and Biff's tough guy act was back on display. "Tell him to dream on! I will not ask him," he declared.

"Come on, man, seriously?" I asked.

"Dead serious! We don't need a silly soccer player that bad. What a stupid idea! Tell him to forget about it; we don't need him," said Biff.

"Whatever," I replied, standing. I realized there was no way Biff would ever ask Marco to join our team. I walked to my first-hour class discouraged and angry. *Why can't Biff suck up his pride for one week?* He knew we would be a way better team with Marco kicking for us. As much as he wanted to win, his pride was getting in the way.

I sat at my desk, contemplating how to tell Marco. I was bummed that Biff had handled Marco's request that way. I was really hoping this invitation could help the issues between Biff and me, but his response had only made it worse.

After first hour ended, I walked back to my locker to grab my science book and lab booklet.

"Hey, Tank!" I turned to see Marco standing near my locker.

"What's up, Marco?"

"Do I need to show up today for football practice?" he asked.

I sighed.

"Didn't go well, I take it," said Marco.

"Not the way I hoped," I answered.

Marco didn't look surprised. "I wondered how he would react. It's no big deal," he said.

"Actually, Marco, it is. We really need you for Thursday's game versus Hickman," I said.

"Well, I had another idea after you left the arcade," said Marco.

"Okay, I am open to just about anything if you will play," I said.

"If I play American football with you, will you play *my* football with me?" he asked.

"You want me to play football with you?"

"I will play your football…if you will agree to play mine," he said.

Soccer? He wanted me to play soccer?

-26-

Having Marco kick on our football team made so much sense. In gym class, I saw him kicking the football and was amazed at how far he could kick with incredible accuracy. We were in desperate need of a kicker, and he had an incredible leg.

He had kicked several long field goals; his longest was thirty-five yards. An extra point would be an easy chip shot for Marco.

But what can I possibly add to the soccer team?

"You want me to play soccer?" I asked in amazement.

"Yes, I will play in your game Thursday if you play in our game on Saturday," said Marco.

The soccer game had been moved from

Wednesday to Saturday because Hickman had a scheduling conflict with their spring band concert. I had planned on going to the game to cheer on our soccer team but playing in it was a different matter.

"I have no idea how to play soccer—none. At least you have a skill that makes you valuable to our football team," I said.

"Tank, on a team, *everyone* is important," said Marco.

"If you play for us on Thursday, I promise to be on the soccer team Saturday," I agreed.

At that moment I officially became a Golden Tornado soccer player—at least for one week. We also agreed that if we were joining each other's teams, we would each go to practice that week with both teams. Marco said he would practice with the football team for the first half hour then leave for his soccer team practice.

I, in turn, would practice with the football team and leave a half hour before the end of football practice to go to the soccer team's practice. I

The Game Changer

agreed, knov ing Coach Carter would let me, since he was the one scheming to bring Marco onto our football team.

We decided not to mention our agreement to anyone, with the exception of our coaches. The weekend was going to give us a good chance to hang out and stay away from any drama. Monday afternoon would be a different story.

I will never forget the look on some of our teammates' faces when Marco jogged out in full pads, wearing a football helmet. Even though Marco's joining the team as a kicker was Biff's idea, Biff looked surprised to see him dressed out.

I watched as Coach Green explained to Marco how to kick off a football tee. Within minutes, Marco was booming deep field goals just like he had in gym class. He didn't need much more instruction than to kick it hard and straight. Following that directive was easy for him. After all, he had been kicking a ball since he was four years old. The only difference was instead of kicking a black and white round ball, now he was kicking a brown oval ball.

The entire team was impressed as they watched Marco booming the football. His ability gave all of us a new sense of confidence. Now our kicking game was like the rest of our football team: elite.

Marco left practice as quickly as he had come. True to his word, thirty minutes into practice he was gone. The last I saw of him, he was handing all his pads to Coach and jogging toward the soccer field.

I knew his position as a kicker would be the easiest part of this entire deal.

Why? Because he was an immediate help, a plug to fill a huge hole in our team. Jimmy would be relieved that he wouldn't have to kick anymore. Even after all the drama, everyone on our team and in Union City wanted to beat the Hickman Hoosiers on Thursday night. Marco was going to help us do exactly that.

The rest of practice I was locked in and focused on preparing for Hickman.

The Game Changer

I had lost track of time until I heard Coach Carter's voice. "Tank! Tank, I think you need to leave," he said.

Our entire offense stopped and watched me as I jogged over and handed him my helmet and pads.

At first, the guys must have thought I had an appointment or something. I took off toward the soccer field and turned back for one last look. All the guys on the football team were staring at me in shock. They had no idea why I was running toward the soccer field.

I'm sure they couldn't believe that their star lineman had left football practice early to go join the soccer practice.

Truthfully, I was in shock myself.

-27-

The jog to the soccer practice was short, and I felt even more eyes on me when I finally arrived at the field.

Coach Newton, the soccer coach, quickly blew his whistle as the team gathered around.

"Boys, you all know Tank. This week he is going to join us and be part of our team. Please make him feel welcome," he said. The boys excitedly cheered that I would be joining them this week. The Hickman game was as huge for them as it was for the football team. I was just happy that they were glad I was joining the soccer team.

I had no plans to play in the game. I figured they would only need my leadership skills and positivity to cheer them on from the sideline. My size wasn't ideal for soccer; I definitely had the body build of an offensive lineman.

"Tank, as I was thinking about the game this weekend, an idea hit me," said Coach Newton.

"That's scary, Coach," I said with a smile.

"I think I'll have you try playing goalie," he said.

I nodded. *That was the best news I could have heard.* I was much slower than those soccer boys, and I knew my legs wouldn't help them much in practice. But I could definitely try to stop some of their kicks if that would help them prepare for Hickman.

They already had Chris, who other than the Martin game, was an excellent goalie. Their backup goalie was a sophomore named Terry Edwards. I thought Coach's idea sounded perfect, especially since they already had two goalies in front of me.

"Sure, just tell me what to do," I said.

"Tank, I've watched you play football. I know you have quick hands and feet, and you're mentally tough. Come with me to the goalie net. This net is eight feet by twenty-four feet. Your main job is to make sure the ball doesn't go past you into the net. Sound easy enough?" Coach asked with a grin.

I stood inside the goal and looked around. The net seemed so huge now.

"All I have to do is stop that small ball from being kicked into this huge net?" I questioned.

My appreciation for soccer grew by leaps and bounds at that moment. I had seen how hard Marco could kick the ball, and it was difficult to imagine trying to cover this entire space and stopping fast kicks like his.

"Tank, think of it like this. In football, your main job is to block the guy from the other team. Well, your main job as a goalie is to prevent your opponent's ball from getting into our net. How you do that is up to you. You can use your hands, your head, or even your feet. All you have to do is block the ball from going in," he said, holding up the white-and-black soccer ball.

He paired me with Chris and Terry. We

worked on some goalie drills. Chris taught me how to move around the net and when to pick up the ball.

Fortunately for me, unlike other positions on the soccer field, the goalie can pick up the ball.

That first night of practice, I was terrible. I tripped and fell over myself, missing almost every ball that came my way.

I felt out of place on the soccer field. Although I was used to everyone staring at me because of my size, it was even worse next to the soccer players. On the soccer field I stood out even worse. A quick glance around made it obvious that I was the only player even close to my size.

Guys built like me were born for the *American* football field. But if Marco was going to assist my team to help us win, then I planned on doing the same for the soccer team.

Marco would use his leg, and I would use my mind and heart, cheering on our soccer team to victory from the sidelines.

After Monday's practice, it was obvious that I

wouldn't play a second in Saturday's soccer game, and I was good with that.

Finishing up soccer practice, I limped my way back toward the locker room. Nothing was easy about soccer, even playing goalie. Those boys kicked that ball so hard, and there was a lot more lateral movement than I was used to. Twenty-four feet might not seem like much, but when you're moving constantly, it can be exhausting, not to mention the bruises from all the body shots I took!

It was easy to see what high-level athletes soccer players were after a practice like that.

When Mom arrived to pick me up, I was waiting outside by the bike rack. Most of the kids had already been picked up; my mom was running late.

"Hey, Tank," I heard a loud voice trailing behind me. I turned to see Biff and Eddie.

"Yeah," I said.

"I guess you finally got what you wanted this whole time," said Biff.

"Oh, yeah, and what's that?" I asked.

The Game Changer

"You officially made the switch. You'll look really great on the soccer field," he said, laughing.

I turned around and ignored him. I wouldn't have had to do any of this if Biff wasn't so stubborn. Now he was making fun of me for trying to help our team.

"That's what you don't get, Biff. I'm a football player, now I'm just playing a different kind of football," I said.

"Good luck, *soccer star*," Biff jeered.

-28-

The week we play Hickman is always a big one for our entire school. After all, they are our biggest rivals and usually our stiffest competition.

Playing would be extra crazy for me this year. I needed to go to both football and soccer practice. By now the whole school knew about the agreement between Marco and me.

Being league champions was always our goal, and surprisingly, even with an early season loss, we still had a chance to keep the tradition alive at Union City. This would be our sixth consecutive year as league champions. Sharing that distinction with other schools didn't matter to me; I just wanted to be one of the teams named league champs.

The Game Changer

On the soccer side of things, a win would mean our school had taken the championship for the first time ever. What could be cooler than both school teams beating Hickman and becoming double league champs!

The week leading up to the game was a blur. Between learning all of my football assignments and the basics of the game of soccer, I barely had time to think.

By the time Wednesday came, I was past ready to suit up and play in the football game against Hickman.

I also couldn't wait to finalize my arrangement with Marco and the soccer team by dressing out for Saturday's soccer game. I was actually enjoying learning about soccer, and I liked hanging out with the guys, but honestly, I wanted this soccer switch to end. Going to school and two practices everyday was a lot for an eighth grader.

Marco seemed to take the situation all in stride. The kicking was easy for him; his only difficulty was getting used to wearing a football helmet.

Learning how technical the sport of soccer is was amazing. I always thought the players ran around the field until someone kicked the ball in and scored. Pretty simple, right?

How wrong I was! I now understood that being good at soccer requires patience, a good strategy, and a ton of skill.

Wednesday's football practice was very different. We simply walked through our game plan against Hickman. No hitting and very little conditioning always make the practice before a game easy. We were as ready as we could be to take on the Hoosiers. I felt good when I left the football field to go to soccer practice. Our team seemed focused, and Marco gave us an extra nod of confidence.

At the end of soccer practice, Coach Newton gave an incredible speech. He talked about what it meant to be part of a team and how important every single person on the team was. When he finished, he thanked me for all of my hard work and said that tomorrow all the soccer players would be there cheering on the football team. Although

The Game Changer

I was a little embarrassed to be the center of attention, it was gratifying to know that all my new teammates would be there cheering on the football team.

As we were leaving, Marco approached me. "You're getting better," he said.

"Thanks, but I don't think I am. Marco, this game is much harder than I ever thought it would be."

"Football is football," Marco said with a smile.

"Marco, are you ready for tomorrow?"

"Yes, it's easy to kick, though it's not easy to kick while wearing a heavy helmet," he said.

We both laughed. On the ride home, I looked out the car window, reflecting on the school year thus far. So much had happened during my first two months of eighth grade.

Not only did I make some new friends, but I also learned a new sport, and now had the opportunity to be part of two league championships!

Then a terrifying thought hit me. *What if we only win one? What if Marco helps us win the football game and then we lose the soccer game? Can we really win both games this week? Suddenly I felt the pressure of having two championship games in the same week.*

By the end of the week, we could be 0-2 for league championships. Will that be my legacy at Union City Middle School? I really don't want Marco and me to be the only two guys to ever lose two championships in one week.

Fear and doubt started to creep into my mind. I had to replace these negative fears with positive thoughts. The stress was overwhelming.

-29-

Thursday might have been the slowest day of my life. The school was decorated, and everyone was wearing Golden Tornado gear. The level of excitement was through the roof. Still, waiting all day for game time while sitting in class was painful. I couldn't focus, and all my classes were one big blur.

I searched and found Marco at his locker before school. "Marco, are you ready?" I asked.

"Of course. It's just a game. We will win," he said with certainty.

It might have been just a game for him, but it was so much more for me. I knew we had to win.

"Don't think too much, Tank. Too much thinking

makes you slow. Just play! You are good, very good," encouraged Marco.

Marco's confidence radiated, and I appreciated his words. It was silly being nervous about playing a game I had starred in since the third grade, especially when Marco was so confident after only four days of wearing pads.

Marco, who had played American football for a grand total of four days, was calm and confident.

Shortly before leaving, he said, "What is the worst that could happen? We lose. Life goes on. Antonio's will still have pizza, and we will have fun."

Marco had a good point. If the worst thing that happened was playing our hardest and losing, our friendship would still be intact. There were far bigger problems in the world than a middle school football game.

Marco started walking away, but then he stopped about ten feet from me and turned back around.

"No worries; we will win. The pizza will taste even better after that," he said before disappearing into the crowded hallway.

The Game Changer

School dragged on, and by the time the final bell rang, it felt like I had been there for a week. I was anxious and ready to play football.

The game was scheduled to start at six o'clock. A half hour before the game was to begin, the stands were packed. We always had lots of people at our football games, but never as many people as there were tonight.

When Hickman took the field, it was obvious we were in for a battle. The players were gigantic; a couple of guys were even my size.

Though Marco kept adjusting and fiddling with his helmet, he looked comfortable on the football field. I imagine it must have felt awkward to wear a football helmet for the first time in the eighth grade.

The game did not start off great. We kicked off, and Hickman returned the ball to the fifty-yard line. Not only were the players big, but they were also fast.

On Hickman's third play from scrimmage, they scored on a long pass to their star wide receiver. He was wide open, sprinting past Eddie, who had underestimated his speed. After the team kicked the extra point, we found ourselves down 7-0 in the first two minutes of the game.

After Hickman kicked off, our offense was able to move the ball down the field running to the right side of our offensive line, mostly behind me. Biff and Jeff were accumulating big chunks of yards, and the defense was having a hard time stopping us. After converting on a big fourth-down play, we eventually scored from the one-yard line. Coach sent out Jimmy, who missed the extra point.

I knew Coach was thinking the same thing as the rest of us: maybe it was time to give Marco a shot. Our defense made some adjustments, making it harder for Hickman to move the ball down the field.

The game went back and forth as neither team could move the ball. We went into halftime down 14-6. The mood was positive; we knew we were getting the ball back to start the second half.

Hickman kicked off, and Eddie returned it deep into Hoosier territory. Three plays later Biff rumbled into the end zone for a 15-yard touchdown, making the game 14-12.

The Game Changer

Coach Carter called a time out early in the third quarter. At this point, he knew tying the game would be huge.

"What do you think?" Coach Carter asked me in the huddle.

"I think if we run Biff off tackle to my side, I can get him two yards," I said.

We followed that play exactly. Eddie took the snap, turned, and handed off to Biff. I got really low and pushed my man right into the linebacker. I didn't see Biff score, but I heard it as the crowd roared to life.

The game was now tied 14-14!

The deeper the game went into the fourth quarter, the more it looked like it would end in a tie. By now both teams had made all the proper adjustments and were gridlocked. The defenses were stout, making it nearly impossible to come up with any first downs.

The clock was turning out to be our biggest enemy. A tie worked in favor of Hickman; a tie meant they would be the outright league champions as the only team without a loss. They would sit alone at the top and not have to share the honor with two other schools.

It was obvious from their play calling that Hickman was playing for a tie.

Coach called our last time out with 12 seconds left on the clock. It was now fourth down; all Hickman had to do was punt the ball, and the game would be over.

It looked like winning another championship was over for the Golden Tornadoes.

-30-

"We have to block this kick! If we don't, this game will end in a tie," said Coach.

He grabbed his whiteboard and drew up a play to block the punt.

"Tank and Biff, I want you to clear a path for Eddie. You two need to blow up the offensive lineman and drive him back into the backfield. The upback will have to come down and pick up one of you. When that happens, Eddie, use your speed to split between both guys. You should have a direct shot at the kicker," said Coach.

I glanced back up at the clock.

The ball was on our own 25-yard line. If we blocked the kick, we would have a couple of plays to try to score the game-winning touchdown. The play was a long shot, but we still held a small glimmer of hope.

We ran out of the huddle and lined up just as Coach had drawn up. Right before the snap, Biff turned toward me. The scary look on his face made it clear that no one was going to be able to block him.

We *were* going to block the punt. As soon as the ball was snapped, Biff and I exploded toward the two middle linemen. On impact, one fell down and the other tried to hold both of us back but couldn't.

Eddie surged between us just in time to leap toward the kicker. His arms were extended high, forming a big "X." The football cleared the punter's foot, but Eddie's outstretched arms effectively blocked the kick. The ball rolled toward the sideline.

Scrambling to my feet, I dove directly on the loose ball. We now had the ball on the fifteen-yard line with six seconds left.

The Game Changer

We have a chance to win. My mind raced with the possible pass plays Coach might call. I figured he would draw something up to get the ball into the end zone.

We had only enough time for one play. I watched as Hickman moved most of their guys deep into the end zone. They knew all they had to do was keep us from scoring. If they knocked the ball down, the game would be over.

"Marco! Marco, field goal!" Coach yelled.

"Field goal?" I turned and looked at Biff. He threw up his hands.

One thing I knew for sure. There was no way anyone was going to touch Marco.

"Give him time; give him time!" I yelled as we lined up on the line of scrimmage.

I got set and turned back to look at Marco. He was lined up, fiddling with his chin strap on his football helmet. He looked calm, but I certainly wasn't.

Everything depended on my friend from Spain and his connecting on his first-ever field goal attempt.

Lane Walker

I knew nothing was easy about kicking an extra point—let alone a twenty-seven-yard field goal.

I felt bad for dragging Marco into this high-pressure situation. We couldn't expect him to save us and our season. It was too much pressure, and the kick was too far away.

It's not fair to Marco. I was already thinking of ways to comfort my friend. *What will Biff do after Marco misses?*

Feeling the weight of the Hickman linemen pushing against me was the only way I knew that the ball had been snapped. Everything fell silent as I looked up and watched the football flying end over end through the air.

All the practice and anticipation couldn't have prepared us for this moment.

-31-

The kick sailed and split right down the middle of the field-goal posts. Marco not only made the field goal, but he also made it easily. The kick would have been good from forty yards.

The crowd rushed the field, and chaos ensued.

I was mobbed by some of my classmates, and the feeling was magical. I looked up to see Marco being carried off the field toward the sideline.

As Marco was carried farther away, I could see that Biff and Eddie were the ones carrying him.

Life had come full circle; the bully was now carrying the hero.

Thinking back, I couldn't remember another time in my life when I felt such happiness and harmony. Winning the league last year was really cool—but nothing like this.

After lining up to shake hands with Hickman, several of us stayed on the field. We had just played our last game at Union City Middle School, and we were carrying on the championship tradition.

I tried to find Biff and Marco, but too many people were milling around the school. By the time I made my way into the locker room, both Biff and Eddie had gone home.

Coach Carter was putting away the football equipment and walked over to give me a hug.

"Great game, Tank. I'm so proud of you," he said.

"Thanks, Coach!"

I was emotional and happy; everything had happened so fast. I still could hardly believe we had pulled off the win.

"Good luck trying to top that win," Coach said.

I looked at him in confusion.

"I mean on Saturday. I want to see you guys win but topping tonight's game will be hard," he explained.

THE GAME CHANGER

I was so completely lost in the moment, I had forgotten I still had a soccer game to play on Saturday. My flood of emotions started to shift from pure happiness to a different feeling—one I didn't recognize.

How will I ever be able to help Marco and the soccer team win? Everyone knew Marco was super talented, and we needed him to win. But soccer and me? I brought no skills to the game. I could not imagine a scenario where I would be able to help our soccer team win.

"Oh, I won't play, Coach! There's no way I'll be in the game, but I will be their biggest cheerleader. I would love to beat Hickman twice in one week."

"Well, Tank, just be ready—in case. You are an excellent athlete, and they might need you," he encouraged.

A smirk crept across my face.

What Coach said was nice, but I knew he hadn't even seen me on a soccer field. I was a football player—not a soccer player.

-32-

Friday's soccer practice was short as we walked through some kicking drills and our strategy for the Hickman game. Mostly I stood on the sideline watching and listening.

The athletes on the soccer team were impressive. The way they dribbled and kicked the ball was amazing. I viewed the game of soccer much differently after spending a week practicing with Marco and the team.

Coach Newton put me in as goalie for the last couple of minutes of practice. It didn't go well, but I tried my best. The whistle blew, signaling a water break. Marco jogged over toward me.

"Not bad. You are improving," he said.

The Game Changer

I nodded in appreciation for his compliment, but I didn't feel like I was. I was totally out of my element. I was used to wearing shoulder pads and a helmet—not goalie gloves and shin guards.

But who was I to argue with the guy who had helped us beat Hickman the night before. Plus, Marco had become one of my closest friends.

"Where is Terry?" I asked, taking a big gulp of water. Everyone knew Terry was Chris' backup goalie—not me.

"He has some wedding he had to attend this weekend," said Marco.

"Wait...what did you say?" I asked.

"He's gone; he won't be there tomorrow," answered Marco.

Won't be there?

Marco added with a laugh, "That means you have moved up to second string!"

My heart sank.

I walked over to Coach and asked in a concerned voice, "Is Terry really gone this weekend?"

"Yes," he answered—like Terry's absence was

no big deal. But he could tell by my body language that I was alarmed.

"Don't worry, Tank. I have been a soccer coach for 20 years. During that time, I have had to use a second goalie only a handful of times," said Coach.

He was trying to be reassuring and make me feel better, but it wasn't really helping the twisting feeling in my gut.

"No worries, Tank. Tomorrow is going to be fun," Marco said as he walked by me dribbling a soccer ball. Well, as long as Marco was on our team, we had a good chance of winning. He led the team with his upbeat, positive attitude, and his optimism spread across more than the team; almost the whole town had adopted his outlook.

In Union City football was still popular and my favorite sport, but I didn't have to love football any less to like soccer. Our soccer team, led by Marco, had opened a great number of people's eyes to a new world of sports.

For me, my entire viewpoint on the game of soccer had flipped when I realized how fun and

The Game Changer

amazing the sport really was. That little white and black ball opened my eyes and showed me that athletes come in all kinds of shapes and sizes. Great athletes didn't play only American football.

I sat down on the green grass in the soccer goal. Most of the players had left, so I just stared at the light blue sky above me. I wasn't nervous about tomorrow; I knew that I wasn't going to play. I was happy and proud to be part of the rise of soccer in Union City. I was honored to have friends on the soccer team and to be a close friend to Marco.

In the last couple of months at school, I had gained so much. Our town had experienced something new and radical; Union City was part of a soccer switch. The best part was that I had gained another team of friends.

Tomorrow's soccer game against Hickman was going to cement and finalize a magical season. With Marco leading the charge, Union City was going to win their first league championship.

I was one of the lucky ones. I was going to have a front-row seat to all the action on the sideline.

-33-

I woke up Saturday morning as the warm sun filled my entire room. I had forgotten to close my blinds the night before.

Walking into our kitchen, I poured a bowl of cereal. Mom was already up and walking out the front door with our dog Max. Mom walked Max every morning; they both looked forward to it.

Dad had some business in town to take care of and was already gone, so I was left alone with my thoughts, a huge bowl of sugary cereal, and a body still sore from the football game.

"You ready for your next big game?" Mom asked when she returned with Max.

"As ready as I need to be," I said with a laugh.

The Game Changer

Since the possibility of my playing was so minimal, I had no nerves or anxiety. I simply sat calmly enjoying the rest of my breakfast.

Mom dropped me off at the soccer field around eleven o'clock. The game was scheduled for noon, but Coach wanted us there an hour early to warm up. To my surprise, Hickman was already warming up on the field. As I walked toward our bench, I spotted Marco sitting down, tying his shoes.

"You ready, big guy?" I asked him.

He glanced up and smiled. His relaxed demeanor was a good indicator that Hickman was in big trouble.

During warm-ups, I kept getting distracted. So many people were filing into our soccer stadium. I guess they all wanted to be part of history and witness Union City's first soccer championship.

Our pregame warm-up reminded me again of how difficult the game of soccer was. Before meeting Marco, I had thought soccer was for a bunch of kids who couldn't survive on the football field. But now I knew that soccer was a tough sport; in fact, the game shared a number of similarities with football.

Coach Newton placed me as the goalie for a couple of minutes. I did a little better than I had before, but I struggled. Even though I was an accomplished athlete on the football field, soccer was a different game.

"Thanks for showing up; I know you didn't have to," Marco said as we walked toward the bench. "I know you are just keeping your end of our agreement."

"No, that's not why I'm here," I said.

Marco stopped and turned toward me with a puzzled look on his face.

"I'm here because you're my friend, and I believe in this team. I want to be here to cheer for you as you make history," I said.

"*Amigo,*" he said, smiling as he walked toward the field. I didn't know a great deal of Spanish, but I did know that *amigo* meant "friend."

I walked over to sit on the bench next to a seventh grader named Terrance, who was a talker. He

The Game Changer

would keep me entertained during the game. Plus, like me, Terrance was never going to play in the game.

-34-

The whistle blew, and the soccer championship game officially started.

As I looked around, it seemed like the entire town of Union City was in attendance. Many of the people who went to all the football games were there at the soccer game as well. The students from both Hickman and Union City packed both sides of the bleachers. They were loud as they chanted a variety of soccer cheers.

The atmosphere was electric, full of energy. My front row seat on the bench was the perfect spot from which to watch Marco do what he did best.

I immediately saw that the Hickman players were good—really good. Although Marco was by

The Game Changer

far the best soccer player around, Hickman had a bunch of fast players. The team also had a star of their own, Peyton Willis, who had scored over 30 goals this season. He was well known for his soccer skills.

Marco took several great shots, but their goalie batted the ball out of bounds each time. Many of the Hickman players were much faster than ours, but they didn't have Marco.

Marco was like a bolt of lightning on the soccer field. He raced around, controlling the soccer ball. His skill set was so far beyond that of anyone else on the field.

At the end of the first half, we trailed 3-2. Our middle-school league played two 20-minute halves. The first half had been a battle. Marco scored both of our goals and also played great defense. I didn't even want to think about what the score would have been without him.

Chris did a great job at goalie even though the opposition had scored three goals. The score would have been even more lopsided if he hadn't stopped a one-on-one breakaway goal at the end of the half.

Coach Newton was excited at halftime; he was confident we could overcome Hickman's one goal lead.

The second half was a different story. Both teams went into halftime excited and came out with an emphasis on defense.

With five minutes remaining in the game, the score was still 3-2 in favor of Hickman. I watched anxiously as each second ticked off the clock. Hickman's offense was set up to stall with the ball and keep it away from Marco.

To his credit, Marco never panicked and continued to chase the Hickman players. With two minutes to go in the game, Marco made his move.

While Hickman was spread out playing "keep away," Marco slowed down and hovered near the middle of the field. He watched as Hickman passed the ball around. The center would always fake a kick to the left before turning and kicking it to the right wing. Marco watched the maneuver several

The Game Changer

times, and when the time was right, he accelerated toward his left. He made his move obvious, especially for Hickman's center to see. The center faked toward the right wing, and without looking, turned back to kick it to his left.

He was too slow. Marco had faked, stopped, and sprinted back toward the left wing, stepping in front of the pass. He streaked down the field alone as the clock ticked down. With Marco's speed, there was nothing anyone could do.

It seemed almost unfair as Marco twisted and turned, kicking the ball high to the right corner of the net. Hickman's goalie had no chance at the ball as it ripped past him. The net cracked as the soccer ball slammed in for a goal.

The kick was good! Marco had tied the game with only forty-five seconds remaining!

With only thirty seconds on the clock, the Hickman players attempted to move toward our net, but Marco wasn't going to allow that to happen. He raced back and forth, forcing Hickman to stall out the clock.

The horn bellowed, signaling the end of regulation.

Leaning over to Terrance, I asked, "What happens now?"

"Overtime," he said.

"How long is that?" I asked.

"Five minutes, Tank."

"What happens if we are tied after that?" I asked.

Terrance turned with a grin. "If both teams are tied after overtime, then the real fun starts."

-35-

Overtime was intense and nerve-racking. The first team to score would win the game.

The next five minutes felt like forever. Both teams felt the pressure and played safe soccer. They knew one small mistake could cost their team the game and the championship.

The ball didn't move much, hovering around midfield.

Everyone in the arena was standing, and I was on the edge of my seat. Twice, Marco blasted kicks toward the Hickman goalie. Each time, the Hickman goalie dove and knocked the ball out of the net.

Soon Hickman had a great scoring chance, but

the ball angled right and hit the goalpost, blasting it out of bounds.

After another five minutes of play, the score was still tied at 3-3.

"You ready for some fun?" Terrance asked.

"Ready? I am about to have a heart attack! This whole game has been crazy," I said.

I watched as Coach Newton met the Hickman coach in the middle of the field. The two men talked with the referee.

"They aren't going to flip a coin, are they?" I asked. I was honestly worried that a game like this could end on a chance coin toss.

"No," Terrance said. "Shoot-out," he quickly added.

I didn't know what a shoot-out was, but it sounded exciting. "A shoot-out?" I quickly asked.

"Each team picks five players. Each player has a one-on-one kick versus the goalie. Whoever scores the most goals out of the five kicks will win the game," explained Terrance.

"Wow! That's crazy," I said.

The Game Changer

The coaches were talking and writing down each of the names of the five players for the shoot-out.

Coach Newton walked over and huddled us close.

"Well, boys, you played as well as I could have ever hoped. I'm very proud of you. I want you to know that no matter what happens, you are winners and have made all of Union City proud. But… we might as well win this thing and make history," he said as the team roared with enthusiasm.

Coach named his five players, and Marco was the last one to kick. He went through Hickman's kicking order, and their coach had strategically put Willis last in the shoot-out lineup.

The five players from each of the teams stood at midfield and watched.

Since Hickman was the visiting team, they sent out their kicker first.

I couldn't believe how much pressure was on the kicker and the goalie. The whole stadium was staring as the Hickman player approached the ball.

Lane Walker

"Can he move the ball?" I asked.

"No, it has to stay stationary," Terrance said.

The entire season was going to come down to five guys and the goalie. Whichever team had the most goals after the five kicks won.

-36-

Obviously, the big stage and the resulting nerves were affecting the players. The first Hickman player walked rigidly up to the ball, feeling the pressure of this moment.

As I took note of his actions, I was in no way judging him; I would have been nervous too.

Chris looked quick and confident in the goal.

The tense pause was interrupted as the Hickman player reared back and kicked toward the goal. Chris reacted to the kick and easily knocked the ball away from the net with little effort. Chris was really good; it would take a lot more than a kick like that to get past our goalkeeper.

Tommy Adams was the first kicker for our

team. He was also nervous but not quite as much as the Hickman player. He had a strong leg, and I thought Coach was smart to have him kick first. In practice, I had seen Tommy practicing a stationary kick like this. I knew where he was going with the ball, but thankfully Hickman's goalie didn't.

Tommy kicked, and the ball gained momentum as it flashed through the net in the right corner just out of the goalie's reach.

The crowd erupted as our team took a 1-0 lead in the shoot-out.

Hickman's next kicker evened the score as he boomed a kick that rolled off Chris' fingers and into the goal.

Our second kicker almost whiffed the ball, dribbling an easy one toward the goalie, who bent down and scooped up the erratic kick.

Two players down, and we were tied 1-1.

The next two kickers for our team came up short. One of them was close to scoring, but the ball hit the right corner of the goal and ricocheted back toward the kicker.

The Game Changer

Their third kicker completely missed the net as his ball soared out of bounds, and the next player for Hickman was a big, broad-shouldered boy who looked like a middle linebacker on the football team. His muscular legs appeared to be perfect for kicking. He stared at Chris, slowly backed up three steps, and lined up toward our goal.

He ran with a strong burst in the direction of the ball and hammered it. I had never seen someone kick a soccer ball as hard as he did. The ball exploded off his foot and rocketed toward the net.

Chris tried to anticipate his move, but he wasn't quick enough. The power and force of the kick hurled the ball at Chris. He momentarily hesitated, stutter-stepped, and then found his footing as he tracked the kick toward the net. The ball rose as Chris dove to block it, making solid contact with his hands and knocking it down to the ground. Chris' momentum slammed him into the ground, and he landed awkwardly on the ball. His right foot spun backward.

The ball rolled out from under Chris' foot, stopping inches away from entering the goal!

Chris tried to stand up but fell back down. At first, it didn't look too serious. I fully expected Chris to get up and walk back into the goalie box. But when he began rolling around in pain, holding his ankle. I knew right away that he had sprained his ankle. Chris had stopped the kick from going in, but he had paid a huge price. Obviously, his day was done.

Coach Newton ran out and helped Chris to his feet. Chris couldn't put pressure on his ankle and hopped off with his left arm wrapped around Coach Newton's neck.

The shoot-out was tied at two goals with one kicker from each team left. The championship was going to come down to Marco and Peyton.

I stood staring at Chris as Coach Newton slowly lowered him to the bench. Then Coach turned and looked toward me. "Tank, you're up," he said with a confident grin.

I had never played one second in an official

THE GAME CHANGER

soccer game, and now I was going to have to stop Peyton Willis from scoring for the thirty-first time this year.

This isn't happening...

-37-

I stood up, feeling weak even though I hadn't yet stepped onto the field.

The first person to say something was Marco. "Tank, you got this. I believe in you," he said.

I nodded to make him feel better even though I didn't believe in myself.

The loud crowd turned silent after the injury to Chris. As I walked onto the field toward the goal, cheers erupted. The crowd stood, giving me all their support. This display was Union City supporting their teams. I loved it.

For a second, I wished I could run out of the stadium or go back and hide under the bench. The walk toward the net felt like a trip of several hours.

The Game Changer

"Tank, remember how you blocked for that field goal? Just do the same thing," Marco yelled from across the field.

At first, I didn't know what he meant. Blocking on a football play was easy and comfortable for me. Playing goalie wasn't. I wasn't good at it.

As I thought about what Marco had said about the field goal, a powerful thought hit me. On that last play of the football game, I had given everything I had. I was confident that there was no way someone was going to get through the line and block Marco's kick.

I would have done anything to prevent that from happening. The mindset I had then was the one I needed right now. The fact that I had never played in a soccer game and didn't know what I was doing didn't matter.

What did matter?

I had been given a chance to help my team win, and I needed to do everything I could to stop this last kick.

Offering me a small amount of time to prepare,

I watched Hickman's goalie take the net. Marco was set to kick first.

I stood off to the side behind the goalie net and watched as Marco sailed a perfect kick. The goalie didn't have a chance. Marco's kick spun over and over as the back of the net swayed from the force.

We were up 2-3 in the shoot-out!

All I had to do was stop Peyton's kick, and Union City would be crowned champions.

The frustrated Hickman's goalie punched the ground as the referee picked up the soccer ball. The referee walked it back and placed it down in front of Peyton.

All eyes turned to me as I walked around to enter the goalie box. I tried to block out all the noise as I positioned myself in the middle of the net.

I turned my focus toward Peyton, blocking out the hundreds of people on their feet staring at me.

Suddenly a strange feeling came over me. I felt a cold chill to my left and glanced over in time to see two people walking toward me from the stands.

The Game Changer

Who would move now during one of the tensest times of the game?

I squinted, trying to determine the identity of the two approaching figures. As they came closer, I recognized Biff and Eddie standing directly behind the goal.

Great...

I was already nervous and filled with doubt; now these two were going to make the situation even worse.

-38-

My legs started to shake with anticipation and fear as I stood in the box, knowing that Biff and Eddie were just a few steps behind me.

I told myself to ignore them and to focus only on Peyton. But I couldn't. My mind raced as I glanced one more time at the pair.

I saw Biff mouthing something to me. I prepared my mind to deflect a rude and negative attack. I didn't want to listen, but for some reason I was intrigued to hear what he had to say. A part of me still liked Biff even after his bad attitude toward Marco and still considered him my friend.

Peyton was getting some last-minute advice from his coach, so I decided to glance back again.

The Game Changer

"You got this," Biff yelled.

What? I shook my head in disbelief.

Biff could tell something was up and thought I couldn't hear him, so he shouted again, "Tank, you got this! Do *not* let that ball hit the net!"

"Yeah, you can do this, Tank," Eddie repeated. I could tell by looking at their faces that they were serious.

They were cheering for me, for the soccer team, and for Marco! They wanted us to win the game. Instead of teasing and trying to get me off-track, they were supporting me. I heard them loud and clear.

I turned back to face the kicker. The coach had left the field, and it was just the two of us. I didn't know what Peyton was going to do or where he was going to kick the ball.

I only knew one thing: I was going to do everything I could to stop that ball. My cleats dug into the sod, and I narrowed my focus.

Peyton stood in the center of the field. He was positioned about five steps behind the ball as he took off toward it.

Standing in the center of the goal, I knew I had only two options: I could go either right or left to block the kick.

As Peyton stormed toward the ball, his body language told me he was likely to kick the ball in the same spot as everyone else had. The previous kickers for both teams had all kicked to the left.

Peyton pulled back, and as he did, I heard a familiar voice behind me.

"Right!" yelled Biff.

At that same moment, I dove as fast as I could to my right. Bill's yell had confirmed what my gut had been trying to tell me: Peyton was going to kick the ball to my right—the exact opposite of the way everyone else had kicked.

As I dove, I stretched out as far as I could toward the edge of the net. The kick was so fast and powerful, the ball was a white blur.

A sudden burst of force hit my hands and traveled to my fingers. The impact felt like my arms were being ripped from their sockets.

The soccer ball was deflected off my hands and

The Game Changer

hit the frame of the goal, traveling back down toward me. As I was falling, I turned and punched at the ball with my right hand. Making contact, I pushed the ball out of the goal. I rolled over and watched as students rushed the field.

We won!

Music blared as the Hickman players walked to the sidelines with their heads down.

I looked up to see Marco running toward me in excitement. I finally stood up, but right before he reached me, Biff and Eddie stepped in his way.

Marco stopped abruptly.

Biff extended his hand. "You're an awesome football player, Marco."

Marco immediately responded by shaking Biff's hand.

Union City had been formed as a unification between two railroads, and that day, I realized how fitting our town's name was. All these years later, Union City was still bringing people together.

About the Author

Lane Walker is an award-winning author, educator and highly sought-after speaker. Walker started his career as a fifth grade teacher before transitioning into educational administration, serving as a highly effective principal for over 12 years. He has coached football, basketball and softball.

Lane paid his way through college working as a news and sports reporter for a newspaper. He grew up in a hunting-and-fishing fanatical house, with his owning a taxidermy business.

After college, he combined his love for writing and the outdoors. For the past 20 years, he has been an outdoor writer, publishing over 250 articles in newspapers and magazines.

The Game Changer

Walker's Hometown Hunters Collection won a Moonbeam Bronze Medal for Best Book Series Chapter Books. His second series, The Fishing Chronicles, won a Moonbeam Gold Medal for Best Book Series Chapter Books.

Lane launched a brand-new, sports-themed book collection called Local Legends in the spring of 2022.

Stay tuned! More exciting chapter books by Lane will be released in the future!

Visit:
www.bakkenbooks.com